Robert Reid

Poems, Songs, and Sonnets

Robert Reid

Poems, Songs, and Sonnets

ISBN/EAN: 9783337006761

Printed in Europe, USA, Canada, Australia, Japan

Cover: Foto ©Thomas Meinert / pixelio.de

More available books at **www.hansebooks.com**

Poems, Songs, and Sonnets

BY

ROBERT REID

(ROB WANLOCK)

AUTHOR OF "MOORLAND RHYMES"

———————

ALEXANDER GARDNER

Publisher to Her Majesty the Queen

PAISLEY; AND 26 PATERNOSTER SQUARE, LONDON

1894

TO

Hon. Sir Donald A. Smith, K.C.M.G., M.P.,

HON. PRESIDENT OF THE CALEDONIAN SOCIETY OF MONTREAL,

A REPRESENTATIVE SCOT,

WHOSE LOVE FOR THE OLD LAND MANIFESTS ITSELF ON EVERY
AVAILABLE OCCASION,

THESE

" WOODNOTES WILD "

OF OUR COMMON COUNTRY

-

ARE RESPECTFULLY INSCRIBED

BY

THE AUTHOR.

ROSEHILL,
OUTREMONT, P.Q.,
CANADA,
1894.

B

PREFACE.

By way of Preface to this volume, it may not be unfitting to give the following excerpts from a lecture on Modern Scottish Poetry delivered before the Caledonian Society of Montreal on the evening of Friday, 2nd February, 1894, by Mr. John MacFarlane, author of *Heather and Harebell.* Speaking with some title to treat on the subject as the writer of such lyrics as "The Last Langsyne," "The Bonnie Banks o' Clyde," etc., the lecturer remarked: "In the year 1874, a book was issued from the Dumfries press of John Anderson & Son, under the unpretentious title of *Moorland Rhymes,* which, more than any other that I know of, gives voice and interpretation to the underlying poetry of the Scottish moors. On its appearance, it was hailed as a valuable addition to native literature, and its author, Robert Wanlock (Reid), from the grace and sweetness of his numbers, took at once a front rank place among the minor singers of the day.

A new and genuine note had been struck from the Scottish lyre, and lovers of the hamely Doric recognised

with a thrill of pleasure that although the age of Faëry
had vanished never to return, yet "the bent sae broon"
was still magical with "the lilt o' the laverock and lintie,"
"the perfume o' brier and brume;" and the mystery of
awe still potent to consecrate as by a solemn benediction
the lonely beauty of the hills.

One peculiarity of the verse, apart from its higher
attributes, is its exquisite form—a quality in which the
vernacular poet, as a rule, is not strong. The dedicatory
stanzas are quite as delicately fine as anything to be
found in the dainty filigree work of Andrew Lang or
Austin Dobson. They instantly transport the reader (to
quote the words of another dedication recently famous)
to a land "where about the graves of the martyrs the
whaups are crying—Scottish hearts know how." . . .

Mr. Reid is a native of the little lead-mining village
of Wanlockhead, perched away high up among the
Lowthers, almost at the dividing line or watershed between the shires of Dumfries and Lanark. It takes its
name from the Wanlock burn—hence also the pen-name
of Robert Wanlock. About a mile to the north on the
Lanarkshire side is the twin lead-mining village of
Leadhills, celebrated as being the birthplace of Allan
Ramsay, and where he resided till his fifteenth year.
The district is rich in native song and music, but its
isolation from the outer world is all that even a Thoreau
or a Carlyle in his Craigenputtoch days, could have

desired. So sheer is the ascent approaching from the north, that the door-step of Leadhills parish church is said to be on a level with the top of Tinto or Tintock, only some ten miles distant, and one of the highest mountains in the South of Scotland. Of the two villages, Wanlockhead is, perhaps, the most lonely, and certainly the most "old-world" and unique. Mr. Reid describes it as :—

> " Far frae a' ithers, and stan'in' its lane,
> Like a mitherless laddie left oot in the rain."

He further informs us that

> " There's three months o' bluister tae ilk ane o' sun,
> And the dour nippin' cranreuch's maist aye on the grun."

But the reader is fully conscious that, despite his playful depreciation, the poet loves it as a mother loves her child ; and to any who have visited the locality, his vivid and graphic portraiture of "Wanlock" will recall with talismanic power this beau-ideal small metropolis of the moors. . . . Its environment is markedly sterile, but to atone for the absence of floral and other treasures, there is always the lovely green girdle of hills—"the bonnie hills o' Wanlock"—of which their laureate so fondly sings. . . .

Sometimes, however, tragedy throws its shroud across their bosoms, and the sunshine is shadowed by some pitiful incident, such as the poet portrays in his poem

c

of "Storm-sted." The reign of King Winter, if neither so severe nor so lasting as in Canada, is often signalised by terrific snow-drifts, and it would almost seem as if, in accordance with old superstition, the storm-fiend claimed an annual human victim from among the Lowthers. . . . There is hardly anything more weird in the whole body of Scottish poetry than the lines in which the climax of this tale of a traveller lost in the snow is reached :—

> " But wheest ! what waefu' cry was that
>   Blawn in frae yont the hill,
> When the wild storm had lown't a blink,
>   And a' the glen was still ?
> It soundit like the eerie maen
>   O' some half-waukent thing
> Shot—or the dour blude at the hert
>   Could nerve its brain tae spring ;
> A wild lost yaumer fleein' far
>   Afore the sabbin' blast,
> And drappin' nameless dreid like dew
>   On ilka thing it past.
> Far i' the glen lichts fired at ance,
>   And heids cam' oot tae hear,
> Gin neebors heard the waefu' cry,
>   That fill't theirsel's wi' fear."

Legends of the Covenant have also, as Simpson's *Traditions* will testify, touched with an almost sacred awe these upland moors,—and especially the braes of Enterkin—so that our author as he "speels" to visit Katie's Well is forced to exclaim :—

" What getherin's at the mirk o' nichts,
    When mune or sterns were smoort or dim,
    And a' the misty muirlan' hichts
    Were quiverin' wi' the martyrs' hymn ! "

In the battle for " freedom's sacred cause," as Burns
terms it, it has too long, perhaps, been taken for granted
that the poetic spirit was and is entirely on the one side
—the side of the Jacobites and the Cavaliers. This
conclusion is not quite just. Mr. Reid's beautiful poem
of " Kirkbride" is an instance to the contrary. Only
the other day, a writer in a popular Scottish miscellany
referred to it as one of the finest tributes yet paid to the
memory of those sturdy assertors of civil and religious
liberty—the stern Covenanters. Another poem of
similar import is entitled " Enterkin." Neither of these
pieces are included in *Moorland Rhymes*, but both
possess in a high degree the hall-mark of individuality,
so characteristic of their author's genius, and in any
future edition of his works will be assigned a high, if not
the highest, place. . . .

While to "the seeing eye and the understanding heart,"
the Scottish moorland is instinct with the purest poetry,
it is yet *not quite* the Elysian fields. It has its bleak and
barren side as well, iron-hued with the stern reality of
fact. But the compensations of life amid the most un-
likely surroundings could hardly have been better or
more philosophically set forth than in the poet's "Hame's

aye Hame : or A Lintie's Defence of the Moorland." I remember some years ago, in the course of a summer evening walk and conversation by the banks of the Clyde, the late Robert Tennant, author of "Wee Davy Daylicht," and of the beautiful lines, "'Tis Sweet to Roam by Allander," incorporated by William Black in his delightful story of "Stand Fast, Craig Royston !" after repeating the poem, remarked, that it was one of the few things of which he had an intense desire to have been the author. Linties have not yet "hopped up" the evolution ladder so far as to be capable of articulate speech, but if ever a gifted member of the race breaks forth into words, it might very suitably be in the strain of this dialogue.

Burns, in one of his letters, explains the peculiar effect upon him of the cry of the gray curlew ; and to most Scotsmen "the wheeple o' the whaup," is more moving than the songs of all the nightingales. But to Mr. Reid has been reserved the privilege of enshrining in a complete lyric this "Sentinel of Silence" among the hills. Verses like "The Whaup" haunt the ear with the strange pertinacity of the bird's own cry. .   .   .

Had I not already exceeded "the time limit," I could have wished to convey a few "tit-bits" from such pieces as "Kilmeny's Warning," "A Sprig o' Heather," "The Spirit of The Moor," "The Cairn o' the Hill"—a cairn grown gray in wind and weather—and more particularly from "Something Wrang," a moorland tragedy, or rather a catastrophe, gleaming like a dark tarn amidst the quiet beauty of pastoral life.   Enough, however, has been given to show that a richer vein than that of lead exists among these lonely heights of the South of Scotland. And my task has been well accomplished if for a brief space any have been transported in spirit across the Western Ocean—have heard again "the laich seep-sabbin' o' the burn doon by," when—

> " The win' sae lown,
> Can scrimply gar the stey peat-reek play swirl,
> Abune the herd's auld bield."

Moorland Rhymes, to which the foregoing utterance chiefly refers, has been out of print for the last ten years. To meet the demand of many inquiries for the work, both at home and in America, the present collection of Poems, Songs, and Sonnets, is offered to the public.   It contains what may be considered the riper fruit of the former book, with a large addition of new matter—notably in the Sonnet form.

CONTENTS.

xvi.   *Contents.*

POEMS AND SONGS.

PAGE

THE LOST HOME.

POEMS AND SONGS.

Contents. xix.

MISCELLANEOUS SONNETS.

Contents.

APPENDIX.

Poems, Songs, and Sonnets.

" Land of my sires! what mortal hand
Can e'er untie the filial band
That knits me to thy rugged strand?"

KIRKBRIDE.

[It is related of an old native of this district that the last request
he made while on his deathbed was, " Bury me in Kirkbride, for
there's much of God's redeemed dust lies there ;" and, taking ad-
vantage of the license which all rhymers are apt to arrogate to
themselves, I have put the beautiful words into the mouth of an
old Covenanter, who is supposed to have survived the persecu-
tion.—R.R.]

BURY me in Kirkbride,
    Where the Lord's redeemed anes lie ;
The auld kirkyaird on the grey hillside,
    Under the open sky ;
    Under the open sky,
On the briest o' the braes sae steep,
    And side by side wi' the banes that lie
Streikt there in their hinmaist sleep :
This puir dune body maun sune be dust,
    But it thrills wi' a stoun' o' pride,
To ken it may mix wi' the great and just
    That slumber in thee, Kirkbride.

I

Little o' peace or rest
   Had we, that hae aften stude
Wi' oor face to the foe on the mountain's crest,
   Sheddin' oor dear heart's blude ;
   Sheddin' oor dear heart's blude
For the richts that the Covenant claimed,
   And ready wi' life to mak' language gude
Gin the King or his Kirk we blamed ;
   And aften I thocht in the dismal day
   We'd never see gloamin' tide,
But melt like the cranreuch's rime that lay
   I' the dawin, abune Kirkbride.

But gloamin' fa's at last
   On the dour, dreich, dinsome day,
And the trouble through whilk we hae safely past
   Has left us weary and wae ;
   Has left us weary and wae,
And fain to be laid, limb-free,
   In a dreamless dwawm to be airtit away
To the shores o' the crystal sea ;
Far frae the toil, and the moil, and the murk,
   And the tyrant's curséd pride,
Row'd in a wreath o' the mists that lurk,
   Heaven-sent, aboot auld Kirkbride.

Wheesht ! did the saft win' speak ?
   Or a yaumerin' nicht bird cry ?
Did I dream that a warm haun' touch't my cheek,
   And a winsome face gade by ?
   And a winsome face gade by,

Wi' a far-aff licht in its een,
　A licht that bude come frae the dazzlin' sky,
For it spak' o' the starnies' sheen :
Age may be donart, and dazed and blin',
　But I'se warrant, whate'er betide,
A true heart there made tryst wi' my ain,
　And the tryst-word seemed, Kirkbride.

Hark ! frae the far hill-taps,
　And laich frae the lanesome glen,
Some sweet psalm tune like a late dew draps
　　Its wild notes doun the win' ;
　　Its wild notes doun the win',
Wi' a kent soun' owre my min'
　For we sang't on the muir, a wheen huntit men,
Wi' oor lives in oor haun' langsyne ;
But never a voice can disturb this sang,
　Were it Claver'se in a' his pride,
For it's raised by the Lord's ain ransom'd thrang
　Forgether'd abune Kirkbride.

I hear May Moril's tongue,
　That I wistna to hear again,
And there—'twas the black McMichael's rung
　　Clear in the closin' strain ;
　　Clear in the closin' strain,
Frae his big heart, bauld and true :
　It stirs my saul as in days bygane,
When his gude braidsword he drew :
I needs maun be aff to the muirs ance mair,
　For he'll miss me by his side :

I' the thrang o' the battle I aye was there,
 And sae maun it be in Kirkbride.

Rax me a staff and plaid,
 That in readiness I may be,
And dinna forget that THE BOOK be laid
 Open, across my knee ;
 Open, across my knee,
And a text close by my thoom,
 And tell me true, for I scarce can see,
That the words are, " Lo, I come ; "
Then carry me through at the Cample ford,
 And up by the lang hillside,
And I'll wait for the comin' o' God, the Lord,
 In a neuk o' the auld Kirkbride !

THE AULD GRAY GLEN.

O' a' the glens in Scotland, bonnie Scotland !
  Is there ane amang them a', my lads, tell me gin ye
    ken,
That winna yield the gree at ance tae winsome muirland
    Wanlock,
  The hame o' lichtsome lasses, and o' leal gude-hearted
    men ?
The lawland dales are bonnie, and the hieland hills are
    grand,
  And mony a cantie fisher toon sits smiling by the sea ;
But suld ye search wi' eident care frae pebbled strand
    tae strand
  Ye wadna cross anither neuk that's half sae fair tae
    me,
          As Wanlock, winsome Wanlock !
The pride o' a' the kintra is the Auld Gray Glen.

Fair dawns the spring on Scotland, bonnie Scotland !
  While hill and loch, and muir and glen, avow its witch-
    ing spell ;
And blithely simmer opes its e'e on winsome muirland
    Wanlock.
  When bees begin tae bum abune the heather's burstin'
    bell ;

And oh ! the fragrant autumn hills it's rare to wander
    o'er,
    Wi' some sweet lass beside ye, when the gloamin' haps
        the glen ;
And Nature's winter mantle sparkles wi' its brichtest
    hoar,
    And a' tae please the couthie folk—trig queans and
        canny men
            O' Wanlock, lanesome Wanlock,
Ilk season wears its richest on the Auld Gray Glen.

The men are leal in Scotland, bonnie Scotland !
    Nae maitter whaur ye meet a Scot ye'll fin' him true
        as steel ;
And lealer men ye couldna meet than won in winsome
    Wanlock,
    I carena whaur ye spier for worth, nor wha ye reckon
        leal ;
The lawland lads are sonsie, and the hieland loons are
    stieve,
    But for the chields wha care for nocht commend me
        tae the glen,
Whaur freens can get an open loof, and faes a steekit
    nieve,
    And gin ye watna whaur it is, I'd like tae let ye ken,
            That's Wanlock, sturdy Wanlock !
Big are the hearts and fearless in the Auld Gray Glen.

And, oh, thy lassies, Scotland, bonnie Scotland !
    Weel kens my heart their glamourie has cost it mony
        a stoun' ;

And deeper e'en did never shine than glowed in winsome
 Wanlock,
 And redder lips were never kist, the hale wide warld
  aroun' :
And though they michtna busk themsel's in silks and
 satins fine,
 The plaid gangs wi' the heather, an' they're baith sae
  dear tae me
That I wad wiss nocht better than a year o' life tae tyne,
 And haud anither tryst wi' baith, awa' across the sea,
   In Wanlock, lo'esome Wanlock !
Sweet were the kisses gien me in the Auld Gray Glen.

My heart is sair for Scotland, bonnie Scotland !
 It's unco sair to think that I may see her shores nae
  mair ;
For I ha'e wander'd mony a mile awa' frae winsome
 Wanlock,
 And wha can tell if e'er again I'll roam contented there?
The sea is wide atween us, and the cruel hills are high,
 And black cluds mar my vision, that I canna see the
  shore ;
But though my life be doomed tae pass aneath an alien
 sky
 Aft will my spirit flichter back tae scenes that I adore,
   Tae Wanlock, hamely Wanlock !
Heaven bless the kindly dwellers in the Auld Gray Glen.

National Sonnets.

MY BIRTHRIGHT.

Proud of my sonship, glorying in the name
  Bestowed by thee, though now by thee forgot,
  Dear mother country! shall a kindly Scot
Viewing his fate without one thought of blame
Though disinherited renounce his claim?
Nay, surely, circumstances matter not—
Though far my wanderings and obscure my lot,
Still am I heir to all thy storied fame!
  For me thy sweetest bards have tun'd the lay,
Thy martyrs striven; for me on Bannock's side,
(Ay, and at Flodden) have thy bravest died;
  And shall I fling this priceless dower away,
This precious birthright? Nay! with jealous pride
  I'll guard the treasure till my latest day.

SCOTLAND.

MOUNTAIN and mist, lone glen and murmuring stream,
  The shaggy forest, and the gray hillside—
  These are thy features, Scotland ! these the pride
Of those that love thee,—and thy minstrels' theme.
For partial nature, that denied to thee
  The sun of England and the soil of France,
  Hath clothed thee in the garment of Romance,
That dearer for that dearth thy face might be.
  Proud mother, whose best son with reverence turns
  To greet thee,—land of Wallace, Knox, and Burns—
Thy rugged hills are sacred from the feet
  Of heroes ; and thy bards (a countless throng)
With tuneful tribute make the charm complete—
  Each moor a memory, and each stream a song !

BURNS AND HIGHLAND MARY.

A ROYAL harp hung in Life's palace hall ;
  And one by one, as in and out they strayed,
  The careless guests a fitful music made
Striking its strings : so true the notes did fall,
That whoso heard, straightway for more did call.
  Thus many strains the willing heart essayed,
  As many hands (and some unworthy !) played.
Ah ! but when Love, the master player of all,
  Parting in tears from one fair visitor,
Taught her deft fingers 'mong its chords to twine,—
  The poor dumb instrument, whose soul did stir
With sudden transport—left on earth to pine—
  Yearn'd evermore for the dear hands of her,
Knowing their touch t' have been indeed divine !

BANNOCKBURN.

HERE is the Heart of Scotland : on this plain
   Her quivering pulse stood for a moment still
   While in the shock of Fate she dared fulfil
Her destiny, and a nation's rank maintain.
O brother Scots ! O fellow countrymen !
   If standing by this shrine, ye do not thrill
   With proud emotion—ye are bondsmen still ;
For you this battle has been fought in vain.
The charging squadrons of victorious Bruce
   Toil'd here for you and me : the light which crown'd
Their weary brows was for our common use ;
   For us the treasures that these toilers found.
Then reverently approach, and take your shoes
   From off your feet, for this is holy ground.

CAMERON'S GRAVE IN AIRSMOSS.

LIKE a sweet incense rising to the Lord
   From this lone altar on the moorland gray,
   The hallow'd memories of a bygone day
Hang over Airsmoss ; here the tyrant's sword
Made brave men martyrs, and their graves a shrine ;
   For here the lips of those who that day bled—
   Staining the heather to a deeper red—
Revere them, Scotland ! cherish and revere !
   Base is that son of thine who shuts his eyes
   To the pure merit of that sacrifice :
Ill he deserves the freedom purchased here !
For to this spot our country's glance should turn
As proudly as to glorious Bannockburn !

ON SEEING A PORTRAIT OF CLAVER-HOUSE.

DUNDEE, thy calm proud face and lofty bearing
  Dispel some fancies that had grown in me;
    In that clear index I can plainly see
Love of high deeds, and dreams of mighty daring,
But not one trace of cruelty appearing;
  This, with the thought of thy heroic death
  Closing thy "day's darg"* with thy closing breath
For an unworthy King, would make me sparing
Of aught like censure; but can I forget?
  Can I forget that Scotland links thy name
    With those old cairns upon the mountain side?
Thy hands may be blood-guiltless, yet, oh yet!
  I cannot love thee if I do not blame,
    Better not judge at all; let God decide.

---

* Dundee gave as his reason for leading the clans at Killiecrankie that he wanted to do one "day's darg" for the King his master.

FLODDEN.

In a proud sorrow does fair Scotland's heart
   Yearn over Flodden.   Leave her with her dead :
   Gaze not too keenly at that stricken head,
Lest once again the ready tears should start.
Behold her sitting with white lips apart,
   And in her eyes the grief of tears unshed,
   Like Rachel, mourning, and not comforted ;—
A sad sweet study for the sculptor's art.
But though her life be emptied of all joy,
   Even now her bosom swells with a stern pride
     To see them there,—the monarch from his throne,
The grayhair'd warrior, and the beardless boy,—
   Sleeping like brothers on the mountain side :
     "Till Death !" she sighs, and knows them for her
       own.

BONNIE PRINCE CHARLIE.

Perchance had I been living in thy day,
  O hapless Prince! and felt the witching charm
  And grace of thy bright presence that made warm
And quick old hopes well nigh renounc'd for aye
By many a loyal heart,—perchance, I say,
  Me too the alluring thought had help'd to arm,
  Nerv'd me to shield thy homeless head from harm,
Or for my idol dare th' impending fray.
But in the calm light of this colder day
  With pitying eyes I see thee as thou wert,
Weak and unstable ; all unfit to play—
  In the great game of crowns—a Bruce's part ;
  Poor changeling offshoot from that Lion heart
Who struck and struck, until he cleared his way !

KIRK-O'-FIELD.

UNHAPPY Darnley! Vain, presumptuous boy!
   Thinking to bind that siren to thy side
   With bonds of straw! not thine the hands to guide;
In *her's* thy life is but a broken toy.
What of the night's delights, the amorous joy
   Those sweet lips promised? where the dainty breast
   On which a monarch royally might rest?
Thou sleepest alone; *her*, other thoughts employ.
But hist, she comes; wake, Darnley! laggard, wake!
   Nay, by God's truth, those steps are none of hers;
   Not hers indeed, but of her messengers
Perchance with some sweet word for dear love's sake.
   Ah, fatal love! too late the slumberer stirs;
For him again no earthly dawn shall break.

ABBEY CRAIG.

THE dreams that nestled in a nation's heart
  For five long centuries, the myth-like lay
  And floating legend of that far-off day
Live here in stone ; here at the hand of Art
Take " local habitation," and make part
  Of our bright present tho' of times old and gray ;
  And to the future from this rock will say
How honor'd of thy land, Great chief! thou art.
'Tis well,—though 'twas not needed ; while a hill
  In Scotland lifts its forehead to the sky—
  While with glad voice a stream goes singing by,—
Ay, though hills fall, and every stream be still,
While one free soul lives on in proud content
WALLACE shall never lack a monument !

ROBERT BURNS.

THOSE things alone are great that stand the test
   Of Time ; and only those can long endure
   That ceaseless struggle, whose foundations sure
In some great truth or principle do rest.
All else, lacking this pillar'd strength, at most
   Is but a nine-days' wonder, in the shock
Of changeful years irrevocably lost.
   But if the house be builded on a rock—
The law be framed in justice—or if Art
   Keep tune with Nature when she sings her best,
That lives ; therefore, exult, O Bard ! man's heart
   Is beating in thy song, and while one breast—
Instinct with generous chords, on earth remains,
'Twill thrill—as mine does—to thy matchless strains !

GLENCOE.

ACCURSĒD gorge ! whose thunder-riven peaks
 And storm-scarr'd sides look as if God's own hand
 Thee to a heritage of woe had bann'd :—
Dread valley ! though no more the horrid shrieks
Of midnight murder pierce thy startled gloom ;—
 Yet in the living pain of thy dead face
 Some memories of the awful past we trace,
Its days of sorrow, and its night of doom.
In thy dark precincts, where no light or mirth
 Of Nature comes, 'tis not for man to dwell ;
 Thou shouldst be peopled with the fiends of hell
That wrought thy ruin ; or the outrag'd earth
Furious should rise, and in convulsive throe
Hurl to the void each vestige of Glencoe.

JAMES HOGG,

(The Ettrick Shepherd).

The genial Shepherd! full of boisterous glee
   As any schoolboy; dreamer of fairy dreams,—
   Rapt wanderer by lonely glens and streams,—
More than aught else had he the making o' me.
From earliest childhood 'twas my lot to be
   Charm'd with his music; with the witching gleams
   He caught from Elfland; and his speech, which teems
With rustic mirthfulness, uncurb'd and free.
How like his own sweet mountain lark he seems!
   The homely garb, the lowly-fashioned nest,
   Where all night long the tender parent breast
Warms to his brood; but when the morning's beams
Arouse his soul,—on pinions swift and strong
Soaring, he seeks the realms of deathless song!

"SHE HAS THE EYES OF BURNS."

On learning that the great-grand-daughter of Robert Burns (who is said to have the poet's eyes) refused to be put on exhibition at the World's Fair.

"SHE has the eyes of Burns," they say ; those great
    Proud orbs of his that blazed with lofty scorn
    When meanness woke their fires ; or teardrops (born
Of human pity), fill'd to hear narrate
Some tale of wretchedness : O priceless dower !
    O starlike gems a queen might yearn to gain !
    O noble heritage ! not given in vain
To one unconscious of their pride and power.
And much, dear girl, it pleases me to see
    That native independence in thee dwell,
    Which, scorning sordid gain, disdains to sell
Those matchless glances for a paltry fee :
    This, more than accident of eyes or name,
    Tells me whose blood is throbbing in thy frame !

WALLACE AT STIRLING BRIDGE.

COLOSSAL shape ! half hidden in the gloom
   Of murky centuries, through which we strain
   Pride-quicken'd eyes in keen attempts to gain
A clearer vision of the forms that loom
In that far distance ; pigmies in hosts are there
   Unknown, unnoted ; but thy Godlike form
   Towers majestic through the hurtling storm
Of battle : lo ! thy terrible arm is bare,
Dealing destruction on thy country's foes ;
   With swelling hearts we view its matchless force
   Sweep all before it in its glorious course :
And as the tyrant reels beneath its blows—
Thy visor up—almost we can descry
The deathless sorrow in thy steadfast eye.

OTTERBOURNE.

Ho ! strike the harp for thrilling deeds of weir ;
 Chant loud the glories of a day gone by :
 Praise for the victors ! nor suppress a sigh
For the brave foemen that were humbled here.
Well are they worthy of both song and tear !
 For never on tented field where banners fly
 More dauntless daring, more achievements high
Crown'd the stern wielders of the sword and spear.
 Proud is each country of that knightly fray !
 So keen for glory, that the victor's bay
Scarcely will either to the other yield :
 But wherefore doubt the issue of the day ?
 Since England's chief was captive borne away,
And our dead Douglas held the hard-won field.

HOGG.

LIFT up thy radiant welcome, Scotland! here
   In lowly garb one of thy truest sons
   Is bent before thee; love of country runs
Not stronger in the peasant or the peer
Than in the heart of him thy laggard pride
   Is slow to own.   And if true love like his,
   And the rich welling of such music is
Lost on thy parent ear—what cave will hide
The unnoticed strains my feebler spirit sings
   For love of thee?   Insulted Coila yearns
To see him seated on the throne that springs
   At the high footstool of his master, Burns;
Then grant the boon, and let affection see
Thy ploughman and thy shepherd knee by knee!

BLUEBELLS.

WE note the standard of a nation's mind
   In England's queenly rose ; it breathes of power
   And beauty, pride, and all the generous dower
Of lavish nature, and is meet to bind
Among the tresses on a regal brow.
   Strange, then, that roses only bloom for me
   As fairest flowers ; they move me as the free
And kindling glance of beauty moves me now,
Wedded to her I love, no more ; but thou,
   Bluebell ! scarce seen beside the rose, thou hast
An influence other than the short-lived glow
   Of pencill'd petals, for the slumbering past
Wakes at thy smile, and makes me inly pine
For bonnie Scotland's hills—thy home and mine.

GLOAMING.

THE hinmaist whaup has quat his eerie skirl,
  The flichtering gorcock tae his cover flown ;
    Din dwines athort the muir ; the win' sae lown
Can scrimply gar the stey peat-reek play swirl
Abune the herd's auld bield, or halflins droon
  The laich seep-sabbin' o' the burn doon by,
That deaves the corrie wi' its wilyart croon.
  I wadna niffer sic a glisk—not I—
Here, wi' my fit on ane o' Scotland's hills,
  Heather attour, and the mirk lift owre a',
    For foreign ferly or for unco sight
E'er bragg'd in sang ; mair couthie joy distills
  Frae this than glow'rin' on the tropic daw',
    Or bleezin' splendours o' the norlan' nicht.

LANGSYNE.

"What means Langsyne?" oor fremit comrade spier'd,
   Aboot the turn o' nicht when havers fail,
   And some ane hinted as we raise tae skail
Tae close wi' "Auld Langsyne:" sic joy appeared
In ilka face, sae kindly grew ilk tongue;
   And as the auld dear owrecome tirl'd atween
   Han' gruppit han' sae leal, and frae oor een
Tears fell sae fast—the lad was donart dung.
And though a' nicht his voice amang oor ain
   Had gart the reekit rafters ring wi' glee
   In that auld bield o' his ayont the sea,—
Yet when the Scottish hearts did loup fu' fain
   Tae raise this chorus, little wit could see,
Be Scotsmen wha they micht, that he was nane.

"O bairn!" quo' I, "here in your ain dear hame
   Life snooves awa' sae cannily that ye
   Hae nocht tae grieve for, or wad wis' tae see
E'er alter'd,—sae langsyne is but a name
Tae you and yours; sma' differ wad it prove
   Gin ye were tynin' what ye hae tae fin'
   What ye hae had afore; but tae sic men
As sang e'enoo—langsyne is Scotland, luve,
And youth;—the land that saw them blythe as you;

The lichtsome heart that they maun ken nae mair,
The leal bauld bairntime, free o' cark and care.
Sic sweets as thae, and mony mair I troo—
The wale o' life's few pleasures—ye maun tyne
Afore ye dree the weird o' 'Auld Langsyne.'"

Poems and Songs.

BRUCE'S GRAVE.

MOUNT ROYAL, CANADA.

BRUCE REID.

BORN 1ST MAY—DIED 4TH MAY, 1887.

Early—bright—transient—chaste as morning dew,
He sparkled—was exhaled—and went to heaven.
                    YOUNG'S NIGHT THOUGHTS.

COME not with stern, heroic thought,
   And pride of country pulsing high,
Ye, whom a glorious name has caught
   And stirred to ardour, passing by :
Banish at once the lofty dream
   Engender'd as that name is told ;—
For brave exploits are not my theme,
   Nor memories of the days of old.

Not here the sacred dust is laid
   To Scotland and her sons so dear ;
The iron arm—the kingly head—
   The dauntless heart—are far from here :
In his own land the hero lies,—
   That greater Bruce that made us men,
Whose fame adds lustre to her skies,
   And wakes Romance in every glen.

Well might I sing each manly deed,
　　The furious charge—the mighty blow—
That turn'd the war in time of need,
　　And dealt destruction on the foe;
For deep in every Scottish breast
　　The thought of these must aye abide,
And where a Bruce is laid to rest
　　Must ever thrill his soul with pride.

But, with each patriot impulse check'd,
　　And every stormful thought put by,
Approach this little grave, bedeck'd
　　With flowers, and breathe a tender sigh;
For purity of life may claim—
　　As well as force—memorial tear;
And on the blazing scroll of fame
　　None purer shows than ended here.

'Twas but a little waif of Time
　　The wind blew darkling to our door,
Round-wrapt with love from some sweet clime,
　　And beauty from the Shining Shore;
But while we look'd, and long'd to keep
　　The wondrous stranger for our own
The little life had pass'd to sleep,
　　And with it all our hopes had flown.

Sleep soft, beloved! O sweetly rest,
　　Unvexed by any evil dream;
A little lamb on Christ's own breast,
　　Transfigur'd in th' Eternal beam!

How could I, even in my grief,
　Begrudge thee to those circling arms
That gave thy tender soul relief
　From life, and all its vague alarms?

Now lost alike to hands of thine
　Are all earth's paltry tools and toys;
Enough for them the flowers to twine,
　And pluck the buds of Paradise:
And those wee feet, that could not climb
　The heather hills thy fathers' trod—
Ah! they have scal'd the cliffs sublime
　That tower around the throne of God.

TO MEMORY.

THE age of miracle will never end.
    There is a wonder-worker with me now,
    Whose feats would raise no blush upon the brow
Of old-time conjurors—nay, rather lend
An unclaim'd lustre to each mystic crown.
    What can he do?   He cannot walk through fire
Unharm'd, nor bring the lightning down
    Upon the altar of my soul's desire ;
Nor smite the rock and bid the water flow ;
Nor ever stay the sun and moon, that go
    Chasing each other through the boundless blue—
Lover and lov'd, that never can embrace,
    Forever hopeless, but forever true,
And she with all his passion on her face.

But other powers there be : what have I done,
    Or seen, or felt, or for a moment thought,
    That I could wish another moment brought
Back from the greedy, whelming streams that run
Forever onward through the gloomy land
    Forgetfulness, into the sea of Death ?
O then arise, and with thy magic wand
    (Spirit, or sprite, or what thou wilt, that hath

Thy home within me)—with thy magic wand
Upon the banks of Time's swift river stand,
   And, at my bidding, bid the rushing waves
Roll back, and show me what their depths contain,
   Bitter or sweet—whate'er my fancy craves—
One moment bare it to my gaze again !

What is it I desire ? What should it be—
   Exiled from all I love—but to behold
   The smiles that 1 have seen so oft of old
Upon the faces that are dear to me ?
I will, and it is done. O wondrous power !
   What glamour is like thine ? what fancy spell
In home's sweet circle for a happy hour
   Could on the instant take me thus to dwell ?
The present fades, the city is no more ;
In the dim past I tread another shore :
   The scent of heather from the breezy hill,
And carol of the wild bird, fills the day ;
   While looks of love my soul with rapture fill,
And kindly words,—too soon to die away.

What, gone already ! Art thou gone so soon,
   Bright vision of the well-remember'd past
   That brought me pleasure all too deep to last ?
How quickly was thy soul-bewitching boon
Withdrawn !—as quickly as it came it went ;
   But I have that within me that can lure
Thee back again, therefore I am content,—
   Nay, not content—for thou wilt not endure.

O wizard, thou art mighty, but, alas !
Thy might has limits, and thy wonders pass ;
   And with a sigh I turn from thee to list
Hope's voice soft-stealing on my charmèd ear,
   Whose whispers hint that I shall yet be blest
In seeing all I sit and dream of here.

SONG—COME AND WOO.

A TOWMOND back, abune Bonaw,
  When lint was in the bell,
I heard a bonnie lauchin' lassie
  Singin' to hersel;
  Singin' to hersel sae sweet,
I trow she kentna hoo;
  I leuch to hear the kind invite
She gied the lads to woo.

" The laverock seeks the yird," quo' she,
  " When e'enin' shadows fa',
And close beside his chirpin' dearie
  Dreams the nicht awa';
  Dreams the nicht awa' sae sweet,
They watna how it flew,
  Then, laddie, tak' the laverock's time,
Oh come at e'en and woo!"

A towmond back, abune Bonaw,
  Afore the nicht was gane,
I row'd her in my tartan plaidie,
  Ca'in' her my ain;

Ca'in' her my ain, sae sweet,
She couldna think to rue,
    But aye at ilka smack she speir'd
Hoo I cam' there to woo?

" The laverock seeks the yird," quo' I,
    "When gloamin' skies are grey,
For there he hears his chirpin' dearie
    Chidin' his delay;
    Chidin' his delay, sae sweet,
Just as I listen't you
    Amang the birks abune Bonaw,
When singin' "Come and woo!"

DEDICATION.—TO JOHN MATHIESON REID.

SHORT syne, in the gray o' the dawin',
　Or Wanlock had opent its een,
When barely a muircock was crawin',
　And never a whaup tae be seen ;
When even the laverock was sleepin'
　Abune the burn heids I gade through,
And ilka bit fitroad was dreepin'
　And drookit wi' dew,—

I gethert a hamely wee posie
　O' a' the hill blossoms in prime,
And buskit it trigly and cozy
　Wi' orra bit ravlins o' rhyme :
And kennin that ocht frae that quarter
　Wad gledden yer heart thro' and thro',
I yoked wi' the Musie and gart her
　Address it tae you.

Some bards get their sangs dedicated
　Tae big folk, tae gie them a heeze,
But gyte wad I be gin I waited
　Till big folk took notice o' these—

Wauf glisks o' the muirlan' and mountain,
　　Odd blinks o' the corrie and glen ;
It's little on favours I'm countin'
　　For these frae sic men.

Their coach rumbles on owre the highway,
　　And little its occupants care
What ferlies may lirk in ilk byeway
　　That leads tae the moss and the muir ;
What lilts o' the laverock and linty,
　　What perfume o' brier and broom,
What wiels the wee burn popples intae—
　　Ne'er fashes their thoom.

But you that were bred amang heather,
　　A bird o' the muirs like mysel'—
And aften hae roved them tae gether
　　The primrose and bonnie blue-bell :
Ye ken the lane scene o' ilk ditty,
　　Glengaber, Necony, Glencrieve—
And far in the reek-ridden city
　　Betimes ye may grieve

For a lown cannie oor in the gloamin'
　　Tae breathe the sweet air o' the glens,
And listen the mavis while roamin'
　　Away amang fairy-like dens :
And sae tae mak' short wi' your grievin',
　　As far as sic substitute gangs,
I send you this wab o' my weavin'—
　　This posie o' sangs.

And gin the wild ring o' their measure
    But wauken a thocht in your min'
O' the days when we feastit on pleasure
    I've ne'er kent the like o' sinsyne :
Gin Wanlock be onything dearer
    For ocht I hae mintit or sung,
And heather and bracken lie nearer
    Your heart and your tongue :

Gin the bonnie green howms o' the Mennock
    But ance in the fancy ye see,
Or rest by the linn o' Petrennock
    Heart-eased wi' its auld-warl' glee :—
Thir sangs o' mine bauldly may shaw them
    Though learned folk lichtly them sair :
What care I though critics misca' them ?
    I ettlet nae mair.

WANLOCK.

Did ye ever hear tell o' a lanely wee toon,
Far hid amang hills o' the heather sae broon,
Wi' its hooses reel-rall, keekin' oot at ilk turn,
Like an ill-cuisten crap in the howe o' the burn ;
Ane here and ane there, wi' a fit road atween,
In the daftest construction that ever was seen ?

O there the cauld winter first comes wi' his snaw,
And he likes it sae weel that he's laith tae gae 'wa ;
For there's three months o' bluister tae ilk ane o' sun,
And the dour nippin' cranreuch's maist aye on the grun' :
Ay, whyles the corn's green in the lallans, they say,
Or the hinmaist snaw-wreath dwines awa' on the brae.

Frae mornin' till nicht ye wad tentily gang,
And no hear the cheep o' a hedge-sparrow's sang,
Nae merle at e'enin' his melody starts
Tae wauken the dream in the lassies' bit hearts,
But a corbie's maybe, or some ither as stoor,
Comes by wi' a wauf o' the win' frae the muir.

Then for flow'rs and sicklike, there's juist no sic a thing,
Except a wheen gowans a while in the spring ;

And the twa-three bit busses the bodies ca' trees
Hae an auld-farrant look as they bend in the breeze,
And scarce want the gift o' the gab tae proclaim
They reckon this solitude ocht but their hame.

But, dod, for a' that its a wonderfu' toon,
There's hardly the like o't for parishes roon ;
Though far frae a' neebors, and stannin' its lane,
Like a mitherless laddie left oot in the rain.
Ye'd open yer een, like a gled's tae the mune,
Gin ye kent a' the uncos its offspring hae dune.

For the chiels are as likely a set as ye'd meet
Frae the muir and the glen tae the square and the street ;
Big, buirdly, and bauld, like the hills o' their hame,
And no cruppen doon wi' inherited shame ;
But gaun frae the knee tae their grave in the glen,
Like their faithers afore them, the walins o' men.

And the lassies—preserve us ! I'm fleyt tae begin,
Lest ony auld carles, wi' prejudice blin',
Should ever but hint sic anither wee place
Could brag o' sic beauties in figure and face :
Sae winsome and backward they were, for ye ken
That a' things were backward up there—but the men.

And 'deed, when I think on't, this very complaint
Was likely eneuch the best frien' that they kent,
For in love or in war the maist likely tae speed
Is the ane that first raxes for what he may need ;
A laggard in poortith a lifetime may dwell,
But Providence helps him that's guid tae himsel'.

And let a' the virtues beside it be theirs,
'Twas weel eneuch kent o' thir men o' the muirs,
That blateness or backwardness ne'er was the thing
That keepit them quate when a ploy was in swing ;
They'd face up tae onything comin' tae han',
And fecht for the brag wi' the best in the lan'.

For instance, I've heard o' a parish quite near
That keepit the causey at curlin' ae year,
And, tired o' defeatin' a' comers ablow,
Were braggin' o' gaun tae the mune for a foe,
When some ane suggested the victors suld try
A bout wi' the lads o' the muirlan' gaun by.

They did, and the consequence was that they fun'
They were matcht withoot gaun tae sic far-awa' grun ;
For they left the heich kintra far sadder, we ken,
And wiser, we howp, than they cam' tae the glen,
Wi' their prood Suthron hearts like tae loup frae the shawp,
And their fine balloon journey a' knockit tae jaup.

And that's but a swatch o' the plaiks that they play—
Be it curlin' or quoitin' they carena a strae :
In city or kintra their marrows are few
At ocht that'll bring the reid blude tae the broo ;
And he that wad twine the free saul tae his will
Maun alter his thochts o' the men o' the hill.

And that's no the best o't—for nae bit I've been
Sic hamely, intelligent faces are seen :
Sae little they ken o' the ill warl's ways

That happiness lies like a dream on the braes ;
And the lown cannie life o' the muirlan' gangs by,
The bud that will blossom or lang in the sky.

And better than that—if a better could be—
That howe in the heather is a' things tae me ;
For there I first lookt on the licht o' the day,
Pree'd the first cup o' pleasure unmingled wi' wae,
And slum'd through the years o' my bairntime in glee,
As blithe as the linty that chirm'd on the lea.

There, tae, the first whisper o' heaven did start,
When the gowd dream o' love creepit in on my heart,
And there on the wild heather mountain I roved
Wi' the frien' o' my choice, like a lassie beloved ;
But the tane is forgotten, the tither has fled,
And a licht less will glint on the muirlan' than did.

But O ! there are plenty tae welcome me still
When I follow my heart tae its hame on the hill ;
Leal looks frae the auld, and kind words frae the young,
And the grup o' the han', that says mair than the tongue;
And mony blithe memories wauken in me
Whenever the bloom on the heather I see.

Ye powers that can see through the maskins o' men,
Gin this be a lee, or the contrar' ye ken,
That never by mountain or valley hae I
.Sic glimpses o' gladness and stounins o' joy,
Nae happiness ever beguiles me sae pure
As I pree when the gloamin' comes doon on the muir.

Sangs tell aboot Yarrow and Doon's bonny braes,
The Luggie rows saft in that measure o' Gray's;
Frac Tweed tae the Beauly there's hardly a glen
But brags it has minstrels and rhymes o' its ain :
Yet here's a wee toon never named in their glee,
That's mair than them a' put thegither tae me.

THE SPIRIT OF THE MOOR.

MORTAL.

WHITHER so fast, fair wilding of the mountain?
   'Tis late for such as thou to wander here,
Unguarded, by the lonely wizard fountain
   That bubbles in the moonlight cool and clear:
This is no place to tryst with ardent lover,
   And listen vows, enraptured though they be;
A sweeter spot would thoughtful love discover
   To pass the mellow gloaming hour with thee.
Hath night enwrapt thy maiden soul in glamour,
   That thou shouldst linger here beneath the moon,
Where plovers' wail and curlews' ceaseless clamour
   Do mar the solemn midnight's soothing boon?
If so—a kindred spell hath surely won me
   To gaze upon thy beauteous form, that seems,
With the pale moonbeam raining glory on thee,
   Th' inspiring muse of my poetic dreams.
Were not the days of faery dead for ever
   I'd look for elfin vassals by thy side,
For ne'er on heath or holt, by wood or river,
   Have I beheld such comeliness and pride.
Bright eyes that thrill my being with their brightness,
   Long locks that flutter freely in the wind,

A foot whose firmest step in airy lightness,—
    All speak a spirit bountiful and kind :
Then, if as frank as thou art fair of feature,
    One kiss—I ask it here on bended knee—
The pass-word of a kindly, common nature,
    A bond of mortal faith 'tween thee and me !
We meet upon the mountain wild and lonely
    That never met before on hill or plain,
Thou fair—I fearless—grant me this, this only,
    One little kiss and then we part again !

SPIRIT.

We meet upon the mountain wild and lonely
    That never met before on hill or plain ;
Yet think not that we meet to part, and only
    This kiss shall be for aye between us twain.
Beneath these stars that stud the vault of heaven
    Long have I sought a soul to mate with mine ;
At length unto my weary search is given
    The bliss that makes mortality divine.
Is it not writ in answer to my prayer
    " The first whose voice ye listen is your lord ;
Shun him that fears, he is a false betrayer,
    But take the dauntless mortal at his word."
Men come and go upon this lonely mountain,
    I meet them in the silence and the gloom ;
But one by one they turn them from the fountain,
    And I am left alone to wail my doom :
These eyes that strike within and heat thy being
    Have terrors for thy mates of lesser mould ;

The Spirit of the Moor.

The earthly drags who turn about and fleeing
    Go back into their trammels and their gold ;
Who could not nerve their courage to the stature
    That shrinks not in the company of gods,
But crippled from the partial hand of nature
    Break into dust at death like parchèd clods.
But thou in manly guise and godly spirit,
    Far other future looms ahead for thee ;
A nameless dower of bliss thou shalt inherit,
    Shower'd down upon the barren moor by me.
Yet shrink not—I am little more than mortal,
    Press that soft hand, or kiss that softer brow ;
Thy faltering soul is at Elysium's portal,
    Say will it muster heart and enter now ?

MORTAL.

A spell is on me, viewless bands enthrall me,
    The grosser world is passing from my ken ;
In the far ether fairy voices call me,
    Ethereal music fills the lonely glen :
Sweet maid, I can but stand apart and wonder,
    I know not what to think of this or thee ;
Some charm hath rent forbidden things in sunder,
    Or touched the iris of my sight to see.
A little while—and this bare stretch of mountain
    Was cold beneath the moon's unwarming ray,
And, as I thought, beside the wizard fountain
    Two mortals met upon a lonely way.
The beauty of the one had nerved the other
    To crave the favour of affection's boon—

The chaste kiss of a sister to a brother,
 Given by the sanction of the maiden moon.
But now the mist that dimm'd my gaze is lifted,
 I see thee in thy weirdly robes arrayed,
With beauty wild and wondrous glamour gifted,
 The living semblance of a fairy maid.
I see thee thus : I who can show no token
 That earthly love will evermore be mine ;
The tie that binds me to the world is broken,
 I feel in spirit I am only thine.
I bow before the eyes that so enthrall me,
 I yield thee all the future I can claim ;
Tell me, sweet lady, what my tongue may call thee,
 That on my heart it may impress thy name.

SPIRIT.

I gently pass among the whispering bracken
 That toss their tresses in the morning wind ;
I float along the curlew's call, and waken
 An echo of it in thy musing mind :
I touch thee in the breeze that sweeps the mountain,
 I kiss thee in the mist that clasps the glen,
I murmur to thee in the lonely fountain
 That bubbles in the wild, remote from men.
There is no sight or sound in all the many
 That long have led thee to these lonely ways,
Whether thy fancy rove through hollows fenny,
 Or seek the sunshine of the upper braes—
But doth the charm that thrills thy kindred spirit
 And holds its silent worship firm and sure,

In all its weird variety inherit
   From me, the spirit of the lonely moor.
Long have I watched the simple fondness growing
   That shows the flower of love now owned by thee,
While I, unseen, the chosen seeds was sowing,
   Whose blossom bourgeons out so fair to see.
And never yet hath mortal maid enchanted
   Her chosen champion with bliss so rare,
As to the heart of him is freely granted
   Who lives the spirit's moorland life to share.
I'll still be with thee, quickening into motion
   The tides of song that leap in light and glee ;
Enough if, answering to my warm devotion,
   The murmur of these tides doth breathe of me.

KILMENY'S WARNING.

I FERLIED aft that wit and will
  Suld smoor aneth the gruesome grave,
And hoo nae crank o' mortal skill
  This deidly weird could save.

And whiles I thocht some baulder wing
  Micht cleave the mirk and come again,
Wi' posies o' the floors that spring
  Ayont the midnicht main.

Sae lang this howp my heart had fill'd,
  That howp a demon passion grew;
And late and air I socht and thrill'd
  Tae pruve my fancy true.

And pangt wi' fowth o' fearsome lair,
  I wrocht wi' candle, book, and bell;
Nae moil was hain'd that I could wair
  Tae work the faery spell.

But ane by ane ilk rede was thrawn,
  The wab I warpit wadna weave;
And fient an icker rowthly sawn
  Cam' stowlins tae the sieve.

Then tae the airts I bann't the book,
  And oot I sten't in thrawart dule,
Tae streak me in some lanesome neuk,
  And geck at fate, and snool.

Or, aiblins, doon the jinkin' burn,
  I'd dauner when the mune was fu',
Where halflin swankies blithely turn
  Tae sport wi' them they lo'e.

And this I lo'ed and grient tae grip,
  Cam' never till the sun was low ;
Nor or the whitely mune was up,
  And a' was lown ablow.

Syne in the toom or dernest shaw,
  Through a' the eerie oors o' e'en,
I'd watch until the mornin' daw
  Tae see the fatal green.

But never glisk o' faery face,
  Nor morrice dance, nor witchin' spell,
Could I wi' a' my watchin' trace
  But this that noo I tell.

And suld the ferlie seem to some
  Nocht better than a daffin' skair,
It maksna, since the voice will come
  Amang oor glens nae mair.

Yestreen, when a' my darg was dune,
    And cankert care had loot me be,
I left yon waukrife, wastlin' toon,
    Kilmeny's grave tae see.

Sae lown a gloamin' seldom creeps
    Atween the darkness and the day,
Sic eldritch light but seldom steeps
    The warlock's eerie brae.

By this I guess'd that verra nicht
    The morrice wad be danced again,
And ettled weel tae see the sicht
    Kilmeny saw alane.

The lift, a' whaur the sun had fa'n,
    Was reider than the burstit rose,
Though east and wast thegither drawn
    Begoud in murk tae close.

Yon hill, athort its yethert broo,
    Yet woo't the glint sae wae tae lea',
And doon this dowie hollow threw
    Its shade on burn and tree.

Lane muirlan' music fillt the air—
    Sae sweet tae me, that seldom heard
But orra liltins here and there
    O' lamb, or bee, or bird.

On ilka cairn the lintie sang,
  Frae spretty cleuchs the grey curlew,
And wilyart muircocks birr'd alang,
  And clapp'd their wings, and crew.

I couldna lowse the witchin' spell
  The time and place thegither brung,
It seem't the verra scene itsel'
  The shepherd poet sung.

Sae there, aneth the hoary haw,
  And as the win' was lownin' doon,
And gloamin' had begoud to draw
  A rowk owre sicht and soun',

I lay and croon't the bonnie sang—
  Hoo sweet Kilmeny left her hame,
And hoo her minny grat sae lang
  Tae see her clear o' blame.

Sma' need had I tae spell and glow'r ;
  It's lang sin' first it drew my min',
And aft I've rhymed it owre and owre
  In mony a glen sin' syne.

The glamour't lass—the minny's dule—
  The aftercome—I min't it a' ;
And thocht cam' thick as drift at Yule
  Aneth that hoary haw ;

Till ane by ane ilk sicht and soun'
    Turn'd unco tae my dwaumin' brain,
And licht and landscape grew aroun'
    O' ither warlds again.

Here where the mawkin, houn'd wi' fear,
    Gaed like a glouf the bracken through,
Uncanny feet begoud tae steer,
    And cantrip din tae brew ;

An awsome wecht o' nameless dreid
    Cam' like a mist attour my ken,
And aft I win't tae break this threid
    O' craft and breathe again ;

Till, pile by pile, on howm and hill,
    The soughin' sprett took maik and tongue,
And in the gloamin' lown and shill
    This elfish lay was sung :—

" Alake ! alake ! sair weird tae dree
    Has he that wons the warlock's name ;
The licht o' life maun quat his ee,
    The look o' yird his frame.

" His heart maun shrivel like a threid
    That's held abune the ingle lowe,
And warplet roon' wi' en'less dreid
    His donart senses row.

" Men wat the land o' thocht is fair,
　　And fain wad lichtly come and gang,
Yet reckna o' the waefu' care
　　Oor ilka joy maun stang.

" Ne'er was a rose withoot a brier—
　　The bonnier floo'r the faircer thorn
For ilk guffaw some waefu' tear
　　Maun fa' afore the morn.

" Then haud by what ye hae tae tyne—
　　Haud weel by it, and want nae mair :
Ye'd aiblins rue fu' soothly syne
　　Ye meddl't warlocks' ware."

STORM-STED.

'TWAS twal o'clock—a gurly nicht—
    The shilpit mune rade high,
Deep-wadin' through a scoury brugh
    Wi' no a starnie by;
Atween and Wanlock hills the snaw
    Gade swirlin' by like stoure,
And like a spell its glamour fell
    Athort the mirksome muir.
A' efternune the feathery flecks
    Cam' flichterin' through the air,
Wi' scarce a wauf o' win' tae drift
    The whiteness here nor there;
But or the blude reid sun had fa'n
    Aneth Glengaber's broo,
A norlan' blast begoud tae blaw
    Wad chill't ye thro' and thro',
And as I barr't the ootmaist door,
    And hapt me fiel and warm,
I maistly grat that ane I lo'ed
    Micht still be in the storm.

But no—I kent that couldna be,
    The wild sea sail was by,
My lang-lost lad was safe on shore,
    His vessel high and dry.

Twa days at maist wad join the hearts
    That Providence had spared
Tae pree a wee sowp o' the joy
    That's wi' the lichtsome shared :
Twa wee short days—sune micht they slip !
    A' days were lang tae me
That lay atween my langin' airms,
    O Davy lad, and thee.
The day ne'er broke I didna miss
    Your fit beside the streams,
And ilka nicht wi' hungry lip
    I kist ye in my dreams.
But sune the weary oors wad pass
    That keepit us in pain,
And big wi' thocht o' comin' joy
    My heart bude greet again.

But wheesht ! what waefu' cry was that
    Blawn in frae yont the hill,
When the wild storm had lown't a blink,
    And a' the glen was still ?
It soundit like the eerie maen
    O' some half-waukent thing
Shot—or the dour blude at the heart
    Could nerve its brain tae spring ;
A wild lost yaumer fleein' far
    Afore the sabbin' blast,
And drappin' nameless dreid like dew
    On ilka thing it past.
Far i' the glen lichts fired at ance
    And heids cam oot tae hear

Gin neebors heard the waefu' cry
  That fillt theirsels wi' fear ;
And ane by ane they ferlied there
  What that sad wail could be
That shook their hearts wi' tremblin'
  As the tempest shakes the tree.

Again—my God ! a human voice
  In agony and fear—
A human voice—it took nae skill
  The mournfu' truth tae hear.
Abune the roarin' o' the blast
  The voice cam lood and shill,
Some nichtit traveller, storm-sted,
  Was lairt ayont the hill.
Lichts sune were got, and bauld men oot,
  But a' their skill was vain ;
They listent laigh and gleg, and socht
  By hill and stream and plain ;
But never mair they heard the voice
  Had thrillt them tae the core,
And ane by ane they a' returned
  Forjeskit frae the muir.
And then we kent the ruthless snaw
  Had smoort him bye oor ken,
And there he'd lie until the Spring
  Had cleart the driftit glen.

The snaw lay lang that weary year,
  But lang afore it thow'd

I kent the name o' him that lay
   Aneth its spotless shroud :
Days past and Davy camena—days
   O' fearsome thocht tae me,
And ilka ane that broke I wist
   Micht be the last I'd see :
I couldna bide in hoose or hauld,
   But wandert far and near,
And prayt wi' a' my heart tae God
   That Spring wad but appear,
That I micht see ance mair the lad
   That thol't sae sair for me,
And lay him i' the mools where I
   Hae howp sae sune to be :
The auld kirkyaird ayont the burn
   Where e'enin' shadows fa',
And nicht is never rent in twain
   Wi' voices through the snaw.

O God, that gart the tempest blaw
   That wrocht sae muckle wae,
At the lown turnin' o' the nicht
   I come ance mair tae pray.
Sair hast Thou strucken, but Thy wrath
   Wi' patient heart I bide,
And tae the chastenin' o' Thy rod
   I turn my waukit side.
This bonnie warld o' Thine has tint
   The licht that made it braw,
And fain wad I relinquish it
   For him that's noo awa'.

Tak' me but tae him or the snaw
 Brings back the thochts o' pain
That rise whene'er I see the hills
 In Winter's garb again ;
Tak' me where nevermair the snaw
 'Ill smoor my comin' bliss,
And ither warlds maun yield the joy
 I never kent in this !

TO MY MOTHER

(AFTER FATHER'S DEATH).

How blythe it was in Wanlock, when summer skies were
    fair !
How sweet to roam the Wanlock hills when those we
    lov'd were there !
Now skies are cold, and hills are bare, and those we
    lov'd are gone ;
And Oh, 'tis sad in Wanlock, for those that sit alone.

To sit alone in Wanlock, when all its charm has fled,
To think upon the happy days that all too swiftly sped ;
Hath life a sadder thought than this—borne in on heart
    and brain—
That things have been in Wanlock, that ne'er will be
    again ?

Oh ! ne'er again in Wanlock, beneath the old roof-tree,
Can such a season come to us, so full of life and glee ;
No more, in undiminish'd strength, we'll gather proudly
    there—
That joyous board in Wanlock has now a vacant chair.

A vacant chair in Wanlock, that never can be fill'd,
A noble presence gone for aye, a voice for ever still'd ;
Death's dismal shadow lies across the threshold of that
   door
That stood so wide in Wanlock, to welcome us of yore.

To welcome us in Wanlock, how eager were those eyes
That now are closed to earthly things, and ope but in
   the skies !
How kind the manly voice of him that bade the wan-
   derers come
Back to his hearth in Wanlock, their childhood's happy
   home !

That happy home in Wanlock—where are its inmates
   now ?
In other lands they're wandering, with sadness on each
   brow;
The gloom that shrouds that homestead o'er is in each
   heart as well,
And far away from Wanlock, it is their lot to dwell.

But far away from Wanlock, and parted though we be,
There's still a tie that binds us to the home of infancy;
Though something of the charm hath pass'd that grac'd
   each stream and hill,
Oh, lonely glen of Wanlock, our hearts are with you still!

And, Mother dear, in Wanlock, thy presence is the spell
That draws our hearts to those old hills we long have
   known so well;

The memories of the vanish'd days, the dreams of those
    to be,
And all that hallows Wanlock, are centred now on thee.

The spring will come to Wanlock as in the years gone by,
And smiling summer clothe in beauty moor and moun-
    tain high,
The heather's bursting blooms will fling their fragrance
    on the air—
But what were these, or Wanlock, if thou wert wanting
    there ?

Be strong ! sad heart in Wanlock, thou mourn'st the
    happy past ;
Be happy ! knowing Love will tend thee fondly to the
    last ;
God send His peace to comfort thee, and cheer thee
    with our love,
Till that dark day for Wanlock, when thou art call'd
    above !

KATIE'S WELL.

[A small spring of crystalline purity in the lonely Pass of Enterkin, well known to the natives of these parts, and easily discovered
by any strangers who may essay to climb its rugged but not un-
lovely braes.]

O KATIE, but thy lips are sweet!
    Their caller touch is life tae me,
As, feckless in this mochy heat,
    I bide a blink tae rest by thee.

Wow, but the braes are dour tae spiel;
    And what wi' loupin' hags and burns,
It's richt weel pleased I am tae kneel
    Beside thee till my breath returns.

And restin' here tae feel the calm
    O' this lown glen come owre my min',
While memory lea's me in a dwaum,
    Wi' gowden glints frae auld lang syne.

For, Katie, I am muirlan' born
    And muirlan' bred juist like thysel',
And mony a time I've seen the morn
    Breck bonnie ower this lanesome fell.

Katie's Well.

And gin the gift o' speech were thine,
　It's mair than joyfu' I wad be
Tae streik me in the warm sunshine
　And niffer canny cracks wi' thee.

What wondrous tales I then micht hear,
　Tales that my heart is wae tae tyne,
O' fairies linkin' blithely here,
　And skirlin' in the clear muneshine !

What trysts o' lovers—ages deid —
　Were held aside this glistenin' stream,
Whase liquid wimplin' row'd a threid
　O' glamour through their thochtless dream !

What getherin's at the mirk o' nichts,
　When mune and sterns were smoort or dim,
And a' the misty muirlan' hichts
　Were quiverin' wi' the martyrs' hymn !

What cheeks, wi' different passions fired,
　Hae cule't them in thy crystal wave !
What hearts that reach'd thee wauf and tired
　Turn'd at thy simple magic brave !

Wha kens but Peden's haly lip,
　Or black M'Michael's bearded mou',
At times may hae been fain tae dip
　Where mine but gethert strength enow ?

Or, sin' thy sweets are free as grace,
　E'en Clavers may hae lichtit doon,
Het frae some cantrip deevil's chase,
　And gledly quafft thy proffert boon !

Nae choice has thou o' hynde or peer,
　Or gude or ill thou walest nane ;
A' lips that thirst are welcome here,
　And free tae mak' thy walth their ain.

Herds on the hills, sin' time was young,
　Hae shared their mid-day meals wi' thee,
And mixed the music o' their tongue
　Wi' thy laich croon and en'less glee.

Nor art thou kind tae man alane,
　For ither voices lilt thy praise,
And ither tongues as blythe's my ain
　Aye roose ye tae the listenin' braes.

For scores o' lambs hae left the hill
　The freshness o' thy stream tae share ;
And coontless birds hae drunk their fill,
　And still there's rowth for mony mair.

O winsome well that rins sae clear
　In this far-hid, unheard-o' glen !
'Twas Heaven alane that prankt thee here,
　Sic gift nae ither han' could sen'.

And while the mither hill hauds gude
   Thy siller spring may still be seen ;
A wee fresh drap o' the very blude
   That keeps the heart o' the warld green !

SAINT VALENTINE'S DAY, 1879.

TIME flies—insatiate, cruel Time!
  How like an Ishmaelite he seems
Whose hand is raised in every clime
  'Gainst man and all his deeds and dreams.

Youth loves: Time turns his love to dust:
  Man plots: poor fool! how soon 'tis o'er;
And Age's dreary drivellings must
  In a few days be heard no more.

No power in us can stay his hand;
  Not strength—for where are they of old
Who made might right in every land?
  Gone, like a tale that has been told.

Nor love,—else would not love keep young
  That form that is his bosom's queen,
Revel in songs the dear one sung,
  And make life naught but smiles and sheen?

And would not I, if such could be,
  (Vain thought, we who have felt it, know)
Roll back the tide of Time for thee,
  Dear Mother, thirty years or so?

Then thou wert young, and fair I trow ;
　And on this morn in storm or shine,
Just as thy daughters choose one now,
　Thy heart would own its valentine.

But since I cannot take thee back
　To those sweet days, nor them to thee,
A valentine thou shalt not lack
　If thou wilt claim thy knight in me.

Here as a pledge I send my glove,
　And on my bended knee I swear
No maid this year shall win my love
　Nor token from her hand I'll wear :

But like a true and faithful squire,
　I'll humbly bide thy high behest,
Content to wait on thy desire
　And do whate'er shall please thee best.

THE HINMAIST CRICHTON.

CRICHTON o' Sanquhar had guid braid lan's,
And the feck o' the kintra-side in his han's ;
Frae the brig o' Glenairlie tae Corsincon
There wasna a neuk that he didna own ;
Baith couthie farm toon and herd's lane biel'
Rentit their hauld frae the Laird o' the Peel.

His credit was guid, and his pay nae waur,
His gien word reckont on near and far ;
Nithsdale kentna the man e'er trowed
A differ in Crichton's word frae his gowd ;
But were it a merk or a boddle broon,
The siller was there when the day cam' roon.

Fu' gleg i' the uptak' tae was he,
And a cout's best price at a glisk could see,
Whether he bocht for himsel', or saw
That knaves owrerax'd na the limit o' law ;
At market or fair for a settlin' voice,
Crichton o' Sanquhar was a' men's choice.

And mair than that—he was held the pride
O' the women folk in the hale Nithside ;

Kind tae the eild he had been a' his life,
And blithe could he crack wi' the douce gude wife ;
And the younglin' jauds, were they never sae shy,
Aye buskit their best when the Laird gaed by.

For Crichton o' Sanquhar was sax fit three,
Straucht as a sprout o' the forest tree,
Buirdly and stieve, o' a manly make,
Less like the esh than the lordly aik ;
Firm on his fit, and free in his air,
And the gait o' his gangin' was leesome fair.

In trowth ye wad socht frae the craigs o' Scaur
Tae the laichmaist biel' on the braes o' Daer
Afore ye'd forgether wi' ane like him,
Sae leal in the heart, sae clean in the limb ,
Few were his marrows, and fewer if e'er
His betters were kent, for they badena here.

But the bonniest day that the sun e'er saw
May be gurly and snell or the licht gae wa' ;
And afore his day was amaist began
The Laird o' the Peel was an alter'd man ;
Dowie and dazed wi' a sair heid-hing,
Mair like a doyte than a mortal thing.

And a' folk ferlied—for nane could see
The gruesome weird that he had tae dree ;
Hairst ne'er failed him, craps were gude,
As heich as the Cruffel the auld name stude ;

At tryst or at market he still bure the bell,
And Crichton was Crichton tae a' but himsel'.

But weel I wat there was one that kent
Hoo the runkles grew on a bree sae brent ;
Her glamour had warplet the clear gaun brain,
And wastit his life with a cureless pain.
This curse gang wi' her wherever she be—
May she moop ill-mated, and barren dee !

Nane o' oor Nithsdale kimmers was she
That artit the laird sae far ajee ;
For though he was kind tae them, ilka yin,
And treatit them a' as he wad his kin,
Yet thocht he aye o' his ain degree,
And their honour was dear in his blameless ee.

But a loesome dame frae the border side
He had thocht fu' fain tae hae made his bride ;
Sae wily and slee her lures she laid,
Sae keen wi' her noble victim play'd,
That he, wha ettlet her a' his ain,
Was seldom fasht wi' the lover's pain.

But oh, when he spiert her for her han',
Vowin' he'd mak' her the pride o' the lan',
Guess ye hoo siccan as him could thole,
Wi' the touchy pride o' his moorlan' soul,
When she leuch as merry as blithe could be,
And tauld him—it wisna her ain to gie ?

The Hinmaist Crichton.

Frae that time forrit the laird was dune,
Fey as a nateral aneth the mune ;
He daunert and drave for a while, nae doot,
But his cracks were sma', though he snooved aboot ;
And a' folk kent, if they likit to speak,
That Crichton's tether was ner the streik.

Aweel, ae mornin' the cry got up
The laird had gi'en Sanquhar and a' the slip.
The wuds were trackit, the moorlan's scoor'd,
The deepest wiels o' the Nith explored ;
But trace o' Crichton fand they nane—
And he never was seen in the kintra again.

This was the hinmaist o' that bauld line
That keepit the causey's croon lang syne—
A line in its kintra's memory bricht
En't like a knotless threid i' the nicht,
And a heart nae man ever maistert yet
Dwined tae its deid at a woman's fit.

Ye wha hae love tae gie, look weel
That ye rest your wish wi' a bosom leal ;
Braw braid acres and manly pairts
May dree nocht better than broken hearts,
And a wearifu' blank i' the warl' he'll pruve
That's matcht wi' a lady licht o' love.

6

BACCHANALIAN SONG FOR THE NEW YEAR.

FILL the cup and let it circle
　　Freely round the festive board ;
Night without may storm and darkle,
　　Here her madness is ignored :
For with wine that beads before us
　　What for raving night care we ?
Let us raise the sounding chorus,
　　And be wilder yet than she.

Do not nights like this one strengthen
　　Hearts that long in tears have lain,
And with links of brightness lengthen
　　Memory's reach of rusty chain ?
Life would ne'er be crown'd with pleasure
　　If we let such moments go,
When there's that in every measure
　　Floats us from the reefs of woe.

Wine was made to charm our sadness,
　　Nights like this to own its sway ;
Surely 'twould be worse than madness
　　All its sweets to cast away :

Let it flow as free as ocean !
   And while hand is joined in hand,
We will empty with emotion
   All our cups at Love's command.

Pledge we first the souls departed
   In the year that now is fled ;
Who so base or canker-hearted
   Would not bumper to the dead ?
Those we loved—may heaven bless them !
   They are free from every woe ;
For the rest—we can but wish them
   Firmer friendships where they go.

Pledge we now the living present
   With its mingled shine and shade ;
May these hours we find so pleasant
   Graff'd in memory, never fade ;
Pass the glass, and let it smother
   Petty spleen in royal glee ;
Come, get up, and all together
   Drain it out with three times thee !

Last, with neither roar of pleasure
   Nor in boding silence dumb,
We will fill the brimming measure
   To the year that is to come ;
Ah, my friends ! there is no knowing
   What this future may contain,
But behold, the goblet's flowing—
   Let us drain it out like men.

LAYING BY A LITTLE FOR A RAINY DAY.

HEY, bonnie lads, that are lippen-fou o' siller,
  Ye that trow the lift o' life has ne'er a clud for you ;
But live sae pack wi' Fortune ye're as guid as bairns till
      her,
  And hing upon the dimples o' her mou'.
Haud a wee, my lads, or sairly she'll beguile ye,
  Dinna think a' the year can be as blythe as May ;
But while it's in your pow'r ne'er let your pleasures wile ye
  Frae layin' by a little for a rainy day.

The wild hill bee that ye meet amang the heather,
  Though he sings awa' the simmer in its balmy bell,
Has wit eneugh to guess there's an end to bonnie weather,
  And pangs his winter stores in mony a cell.
Then when the snaw comes, and bitter winds are roarin',
  Little will it fash him suld the drift smoor the brae,
Among his gowden kaims like a king he'll be snorin'—
  His honey has been hoordit for a rainy day.

Far be't frae me e'er to stint the young o' pleasure,
  Aneath its cheery sunshine they are baith guid and
      fair ;

But just a kennin' less in the reamin' daily measure,
　Wad mak' but little differ here or there ;
And gey puir comfort it gies to man or woman
　To ken they've wastit chances they ne'er again can
　　hae,
To see the simmer's pride fa', and dreary winter comin',
　And ken they've naething hoordit for a rainy day.

JEAN : A LYRIC.

Few are the flowers on Wanlock braes,
   And wondrous tiny those that be,
For nights of storm and sunless days
   Keep down their growth on moor and lea ;
But though the hills be stern and bare,
   And flowers are few and far between,
One peerless blossom still is there,
   Rose of the wilds—its name is Jean.

Nursed in this lonely glen, my heart
   Has borne like it few things of joy,
But chiefly lived its life apart
   From love of man and maiden coy ;
But though its golden dreams are rare,
   And in their glow few shapes are seen,
One face forever lingers there—
   One queenly form—its name is Jean.

And Wanlock braes, despite this dearth
   Of leaf and petal, scent and show,
Are dear above all braes on earth
   Where buds of beauty thickly blow ;
Nor does my heart in wailings loud
   Mourn o'er a happier might-have-been,
But dwells apart, content and proud ;
   Would'st know the charm ?—its name is Jean.

GRAVES ON THE SCOTTISH HILLS.

The gloamin' fa's fu' bonnily
 Frae blue Canadian skies,
And at my fit, composed for sleep,
 A queenly city lies ;
Frae stey Mount Royal's rugged crest
 I view the winsome scene,
And mark the stately river rowe
 Its noble width atween :
Blythe sicht it is ! and weel micht be
 The theme o' bardie's lay,
For fairer spot ye wadna see,
 And travel mony a day.

But, lanely as I sit at rest
 Upon the mountain bree,
I see the beauties o' the place,
 And yet I dinna see,
For crowdin' oot the things that are,
 Auld Scotland fills my min' ;
I see the mirk come owre the hills
 I kent sae weel langsyne ;
Dear scenes o' youth wi' fidgin fit,
 And blythe heart loupin' fain,
In a deep dwaum 'tween sense and sleep
 I spiel your hichts again.

O, leese me on the mountain taps,
   And on the grey hill sides ;
And leese me on ilk wimplin' burn
   That doon its forkin' slides ;
And lichtly may the dawin break
   That opens e'en tae see
The lang bare muirs and dowie glens
   Forever dear tae me ;
Where, an' the whaup wad quat his cry,
   And the wee burn be still,
Ye maist wad trow the weird o' doom
   Hung roon ilk hauntit hill !

But be they lown as midnicht,
   Or blythe wi' bird and burn,
What thochts they wauken up in me
   Whichever airt I turn !
Big thochts o' Scotland's glory, won
   Amang her warriors stern,
By him whase banes hae fa'n tae mools
   Aneth yon hoary cairn ;
Yon hoary cairn that like a ghaist
   Glow'rs owre the upland braes,
And tells tae ilka wicht that speirs
   Its tale o' ither days.

There lies the buirdly bouk o' ane
   Wham king could never cowe ;
The heart where Freedom's genty spark
   Brunt wi' a cheery lowe ;

The stalwart airm that redd the road
    When faes were thick and fell !
And the trumpet-tongue that through the storm
    Rang clearer than a bell ;
O, Fame ! is this the gate ye pay
    Debts ye suld blush tae aw' ?
A grey stane on a mountain side,
    And nocht tae tell for wha !

But, wantin' even a stane to tell
    That mortal banes are by,
What disrespeckit grave is this,
    Bare tae the gurly sky ?
O lichtly press the lanely turf !
    It hauds some desperate saul
Wha couldna wait till He that bound
    Released his life frae thrall,
Sae wi' his ain impatient hand
    He took that life awa',
And here in lanely exile bides
    The hinmaist trumpet's ca'.

Nae consecrated burial-place
    His outlaw'd dust could claim,
Nae auld kirk steeple wagg'd its tongue
    When this puir chield wan hame ;
For him nae woman's cheek was wat,
    Nor maiden's e'e was dim ;
The very bairns wad grue wi' dreid,
    And hide when tauld o' him.

Sae by the wan licht o' the mune
   Some twa-three men cam' here,
Syne howkt a hole and hid the deid,
   And hurried hame in fear.

It's said that at the mirk midnight,
   When a'thing else is still,
An eerie soun' is aften heard
   By folk gawn owre the hill—
An eerie soun' o' dule an' dreid
   Like cries o' ane in pain—
And ever and aye comes in between
   The clankin' o' a chain.
I canna tell gin this be true,
   But I've heard the hill folk say
That the herds wad gang five mile aboot
   Tae pass this lanely brae.

Doon in the hollow o' the burn
   A cairn o' stanes ye'll see,
Where, on an awsome winter nicht,
   A stranger lad did dee.
The road was tint, the nicht was mirk,
   The snaw blew thick and snell,
And just a kennin frae the toon
   The weary stranger fell,
Without a freen' tae close his e'e,
   Or hear his pairtin' cry,
God, wha tak's tent when sparrows fa'
   Alane was standin' by.

And see ye yon wee bit benty knowe
 Scarce rais'd abune the yird,
Whase only use wad seem to be
 To rest some weary herd,
And yet a noble martyr lies
 Aneth that grassy sod,
Shot wi' his Bible in his hand,
 There worshippin' his God !
Hill rang tae hill, and glen tae brae,
 When that fell deed was dune ;
But gin ye wad learn the martyr's name,
 It's in the Buik abune.

Fu' mony a nameless grave like this
 Hallows thy hills, Scotland !
Fu' mony a heart that lo'ed thee well
 Lies at thy heart unkenn'd ;
Auld sangs and stories tell o' some,
 And stir our souls wi' pride,
But never sall we ken till doom
 The hoord o' the hale hillside ;
For warrior bauld and coward loon,
 And weary wanderin' chield,
Wi' mony a witness for the truth,
 Sleep in thy kindly beild.

On the bare muir they lie at rest,
 Fause heart and heart as true,
On the muir amang the moss,
 Aneth the lift sae blue,

And owre their heids the linty chirms,
   And the wild plovers cry,
And like the ferlies in a dream,
   The wanderin' win' gangs by.
Wha kens, that hisna heard its sugh,
   Gin nocht but win' be there ?
For whyles I think the hameless deid
   Are yaumerin' through the air.

Tongues o' the deid—wild, waefu' souns—
   Forever haunt the hill ;
Or when the win' is laich and lown,
   Or rairin' lood and shrill.
Abune the scaur or in the howe,
   Alang the breezes borne,
The skraigh o' ilka bird comes by,
   Like speech frae heart forlorn.
And be the lawlands braw wi' trees,
   And prankt wi' mony a floo'r,
For wilder joys than they can yield,
   I seek the ghaistly muir.

My days gang by in exile
   Three thoosan' miles frae hame,
And I've dune nocht for Scotland yet
   Tae hae on her a claim ;
But suld I ever win the richt
   Tae beg ae boon o' her,
I want nae monuments o' stane,
   Nor ocht tae mak' a stir ;

But far awa' amang her hills
   That my dune dust be laid,
Wi' the mist tae settle owre my heid
   And hap me like a plaid !

IN THE GARDEN, OUTREMONT.

I WALK within my garden, at the quiet evening hour,
When all the air hangs heavily with scent of fruit and
    flower ;
While here a bud and there a bloom attract me as I
    stroll,
And Autumn's tranquil loveliness is mirror'd in my soul:
Perchance the silvery moonlight streams athwart each
    branching tree,
And lends its lustrous witchery to every shape I see.
Is it not strange, in such a scene with beauty all aglow,
My heart should seek the rugged hills and haunts of
    long ago ?

Close by, my happy homestead stands, withdrawn in
    umbrage deep,
Where, hours ago, my little ones were wrapt in balmy
    sleep ;
My wife is singing softly as she moves from room to
    room,
Her bright lamp casting lanes of light through all the
    leafy gloom :
I hear her crooning to herself some old subdued refrain,
As though she fear'd to wake to life those noisy imps
    again :—

Why should I turn me from that music welling rich and
    low,
To list the far-off voices and the songs of long ago?

Up there, on steep Mount Royal, where the pine-trees
    darkly wave,
The silent stars look down upon a little tiny grave ;
The winds make music o'er it, and the spot is fair to see,
And oh the dust within that grave is very dear to me !
But though the dust were doubly dear, the spot more
    sweetly fair,
'Twould give me little joy to think I'll one day slumber
    there :
Far liefer would I lay my head where Wanlock's waters
    flow
Around our own God's acre, with the loved of long ago.

Oh Land of misty mountain heights, of lonely glens and
    lakes,
The tie that binds my heart to thee nor time nor distance
    breaks ;
True to the soil that bore me, and the race from which
    I spring
Forever backward o'er the wave to thee my thoughts
    take wing :
Still fairest of all sights to me is morning on thy Bens,
And sweetest sound, the wild bird's note at gloaming in
    thy glens ;
And dearest of all memories, the cherish'd thoughts
    that flow
In solitary hours like these from dreams of long ago.

Scotland ! thou art the shrine to which my partial fancy
    turns,
Land of the hero, seer, and bard, of Wallace, Knox, and
    Burns ;
Land, where my infant eyes first saw the purple heather
    wave ;
Land, where the chilly hill-wind weeps upon my father's
    grave :
Oh ! many charms has Canada, and to my soul 'tis dear,
For all the choicest gifts of time are gather'd round me
    here :
But in my breast the ruddy stream must falter cold and
    slow
Ere I forget dear Scotland, and the days of long ago !

THE WHAUP.

Fu' sweet is the lilt o' the laverock
    Frae the rim o' the clud at morn ;
The merle pipes weel in his mid-day biel',
    In the heart o' the bendin' thorn ;
The blythe, bauld sang o' the mavis
    Rings clear in the gloamin' shaw :
But the whaup's wild cry in the gurly sky
    O' the moorlan' dings them a'.

For what's in the lilt o' the laverock
    Tae touch ocht mair than the ear ?
The merle's lown craik in the tangled brake
    Can start nae memories dear ;
And even the sang o' the mavis
    But waukens a love-dream tame
Tae the whaup's wild cry on the breeze blawn by,
    Like a wanderin' word frae hame.

What thochts o' the lang gray moorlan'
    Start up when I hear that cry !
The times we lay on the heathery brae
    At the well, lang syne gane dry ;

7

And aye as we spak' o' the ferlies
　　That happen'd afore-time there,
The whaup's lane cry on the win' cam' by
　　Like a wild thing tint in the air.

And though I ha'e seen mair ferlies
　　Than grew in the fancy then,
And the gowden gleam o' the boyish dream
　　Has slipp'd frae my soberer brain,
Yet—even yet—if I wander
　　Alane by the moorlan' hill,
That queer wild cry frae the gurly sky
　　Can tirl my heart-strings still.

SONG: THE CONTENTED SHEPHERD.

THE king has a croon, and I hae nane,
  And gin he is prood sae let him be ;
But the wecht o't maun tell on his white hause-bane,
  For he hauds his heid nae heicher than me ;
My pow ne'er yeuks to be ringed wi' gowd,
  But a gude blue bannet can busk it fair,
And I'm blythe on the hill in my grey plaid row'd,
  Div ye think that the king need want ocht mair ?

I come frae the hill when the e'enin'-fa's,
  Gled that the darg o' the day is by ;
And the wee things meet me wi' cheerisome craws,
  And the gudewife smiles when she sees me nigh ,
And a' forenicht by the ingle side
  We fley Daddy Care wi' a royal glee,
For I rule my realms wi' a faitherly pride ;
  Wad ye glow'r gin the king micht swap wi' me ?

In the auld kirkyard ayont the burn
  The grass grows bonnie abune my kin,
And I carena hoo sune it may come my turn
  To hae dune wi' the warld and lie therein ;
I ken that the dust maun turn to dust,
  But never ance fear that the saul may tine ;
For I trust where my forbeirs a' pat their trust :
  Wad the king gie nocht for a faith like mine ?

NECONY.

Roun' by Necony the heather blumes bonnie,
 And sweet is the lilt o' the mosscheiper's sang ;
But though ye'd gang farrer and no fin ocht fairer,
 Yet roun' by Necony I carena tae gang :
I'll rove by Petrennock, Snarswater or Mennock,
 The stey craigs o' Carron I'll still spiel wi' glee ;
But roun' by Necony there's something no canny,
 And he that's no fley'd for't is baulder than me !

I canna tell whether the blume o' the heather
 Be reider owre yonder than heather suld be,
But aye when I see it in blossom, tae me it
 Taks shape like the dreepin o' blude in the ee :
The mosscheiper's liltin', at ither times meltin',
 Gangs thro' the daz'd heart wi' a dirl and a stoun ;
In yaumers sae eerie, wi' naething clse near ye,
 Ye grue as a warlock were raisin' the soon.

But gruin' or glowrin', nocht mair overpow'rin'
 Will stertle the calm on the breist o' the glen ;
Nae warlock or wurricoo bides in Necony noo,
 Scarce can you trace its connection wi' men :
But though they be rotten, their memory forgotten,
 And naething be kent o' their deeds or their doom,
God's mercy, Necony ! there's something no canny
 Has happent tae cleed ye in glamour and gloom.

The Lost Home.

THE LOST HOME.

Summer will deck thy bonnie braes again,
My moorland home ; upon thy shaggy hills
The purple heather—by thy wimpling rills
Bluebell and bracken—will announce its reign.
As bravely as of old the blackcock's note
Will usher in the dawn ; and o' still nights,
E'er gloaming like a mantle wraps thy heights,
From some far glen the mavis' song will float.
But other ears must hear, and other eyes
Behold these things : for unto me they seem
But memories of a sad yet tender dream ;
And thou thyself—a haunted spot that lies
Beyond this earth, in some realm of the dead
Where mortal foot of mine no more may tread.

ON NAMING MY SON WANLOCK.

As if it were not always in my heart,
  Sleeping or waking ; in my quiet room,
Or toiling in the city's busy mart,
  And like a sun-glint ever in the gloom
Lightening my lot—the dream of childhood's home
  With all its lov'd ones ; all its breezy hills,
  Calm glens, lone uplands, myriad murmuring rills,
Whereby no more my exiled feet may roam ;
Out of the fulness of my love for these,
  And that my tongue in speaking it may share
    The untold joy of dreaming—I will give
My boy its name : then though the heartless seas
  Divide me from the old I found so fair,
    In this new Wanlock all my hopes will live.

TO MY MOTHER.

THERE are not many days throughout the year
   In which fond memory does not retrace
   My path of life back to its starting place,—
The little glen that I still hold so dear.
But of all days, and of all objects there,
   This day my warmest thoughts should surely be
   In filial duty centred all on thee,—
Thou object of my heart's sincerest prayer !
Dear Mother ! may the love of all thy sons
   And daughters, now in thy declining years,
Comfort and cheer thee as the season runs,
   And never deed of ours bring any tears
But tears of joy ; let these thy glad eyes fill,
Seeing we honour, love, and prize thee still !

TO THE LOWTHERS.

(AFTER A LONG ABSENCE.)

HAVE ye no voice to welcome my return,
    Nor arms to clasp me to your parent breast,
    O stern, cold hills ! whose every lofty crest
Withdraws to leaden skies in silent scorn ?
Not thus the human mother hails the son,
    Whose feet, from wandering on a foreign shore,
Turn, tired of travel and adventure done,
    To prove the peace of childhood's home once more ;
And ill your gloom requites his glance elate
    Who, leaving fairer scenes beyond the sea,
    (Where of His grace God has been good to me
With health and plenty, wife and children dear,)
Drawn by heart-hunger, seeks no better fate
    Than to be gather'd to his fathers here.

THE REASON WHY.

Not for their beauty do I love the hills
   Of which I sing—fair though the features seem
   Bath'd in the splendour of the morning's beam,
Or clad in that soft witchery that fills
Each glen at gloaming ; not for this the rills
   Are more to me than any classic stream
   That ever Poet chose him for a theme :—
A sweeter reason all my being thrills !
They are my own ! the much-lov'd hills of home
   Not with that earthly ownership which looks
   For rent and taxes ; but because the brooks,
The braes, the glens, all—all—where'er I roam
Have voices sounding in the lonely wild,
That call me as a mother calls her child.

MENNOCK.

Sing on, sweet Mennock, to thy listening hills !
   Far in the moorland where thy stream has birth
   (That dearest spot to me of all the earth)
From many glens thou drawest kindred rills
To swell thy melody : into thy voice
   The music of those moors has pass'd ; the call
   Of lonely birds, the bleat of lambs, and all
The happy sounds that make the wilds rejoice.
Past pleasant holms—growing in beauty still,—
   Skirting the bases of the silent steeps,
   Where at the noontide listless nature sleeps ;
Through wooded gorges that the linnets fill
With answering song—till Nith's fair flood we see—
Sing on, sweet Mennock, to thy hills and me !

CARSEHOPE.

(INSCRIBED TO J. M. R.)

SOMETIMES, when very weary of my lot—
  Tired with the dull routine of city life—
    Seeing the same sights every dismal day,—
Gray houses, dusty streets ; without one spot
  Home-like to cheer me : all my heart at strife
    With its environments, and far away,—
Perch'd at my desk with all the ledgers round,
  I shut my eyes, and this is what I see :—
    A streamlet running 'neath a cloudless sky
    Through mountain solitudes ; two weary men,
    Tired with a long day's ramble (you and I,)
Stretch'd prone beside it, with no harsher sound
  To mar their musings, than the wandering bee
    Makes, as he crosses this enchanted glen.

GLENCRIEVE.

Is this Glencrieve? I deem'd the spot more fair
  When here we linger'd many years ago—
  My love and I—and watch'd the ruddy glow
Of sunset deaden on the moorlands bare.
Perchance my foot some erring path hath ta'en
  That led astray, and I have missed Glenrcrieve :
  Then will I back, for I am loth to leave
These hills, till memory be stirr'd again.
Yet stay ! this is the glen : yon glint so bright
  Smites the long upland and its summit hoar,
    Just as it smote them then ; but I, alone,
Here in the shadow'd gorge, have lost the light
  Of eyes, whose lustre rob'd the scene of yore
    In a dim loveliness for ever flown.

AUCHENLONE.

In the dim gloaming, dreaming of old days,
　　When far-off forms and half-forgotten things
　　　　Take shape again before me in the gloom—
No fairer vision rises to my gaze,
　　Nor sight more welcome wizard Fancy brings,
　　　　Than the last glimpse that in my heart finds room
Of thee, lov'd mountain ; Oh ! for words to show
　　The summer sunlight slanting from the west,
And Enterkin in shadow : all thy braes aglow
　　With heath and thyme, and high above thy crest
One solitary watcher of the glen below
　　Circling and screaming,—all things else at rest :
And my last look—ta'en with an envious thrill—
The great bird settling on his native hill.

ENTERKIN.

SMOOTH rounded peaks rise up on either hand
  In long array; and in between the rills,
  Skirting the bases of the silent hills,
Join each to each as with a silver band.
Morn breaks not on a fairer scene than this
  In beauteous Scotland: peaceful, holy, calm:
  The Lowther zephyr charg'd with summer balm
Steals to my forehead like a mother's kiss.
Enterkin! glen of peace; oft have I bent
  My steps towards thee in a happier day:
  Here in thy praise have conn'd my boyish lay,
My head upon thy turf in sweet content:
And, when the tumult of this life is past,
Here gladly would I lay my head at last.

THE FIRST BREAK.

Sɪᴛ closer, closer, round the darken'd hearth ;
  Let not an eye look to'rd the vacant chair
  We know, alas ! too well, is standing there,
Like a dread presence chilling all our mirth ;—
'Till now the seat of him who gave us birth.
  The stern grey man, the man of toil and prayer,
  In whose rich legacies 'tis ours to share—
Of bright example, and of moral worth.
The first black cloud looms up our summer sky,
  Sad prelude of the dismal days to be,
  And my heart shakes within my breast to see
That other lov'd one—knowing the time is nigh
She too will leave us, and that yearning eye
  Tear-bright with love will look no more on me.

ON READING OF THE EARL OF DALKEITH'S MARRIAGE.

DALKEITH, your wedding bells assail mine ear
  With gladsome music ; gladsome may you be !
  Though my own heart be not from sorrow free,
Yet can it thrill another's joy to hear.
God bless you both ! proud Earl and Fair Ladye !
  Long may you serve your country and your Queen :
  For true to both, your race hath ever been,
And, little doubt, I true 'twill ever be !
But when long service leaves you old and gray
  May you and yours be spared the bitter pain
  We feel, whose sire's life-service could not gain
For our dear mother, in her widow'd day,
The lowly roof Buccleuch might well have given
To shield her till she pass'd from earth to heaven.

OUR MARY IN HEAVEN.

Ah ! my sweet sister, whose young tender feet
　Fail'd on Life's rugged path long years ago,—
　For loss of whom the bitter tears did flow,
Because we deem'd not then rest was so sweet,
Nor how thrice lovely was the bright retreat
　Thy spirit sought ; how would this day of woe
　Have wrung thy gentle heart, that doted so
On home and all that made its charm complete !
But can we doubt that in thy new-found home
　Thy careful hand will have prepared a place
　Where we, the wayworn laggards of thy race,
After this life's probation ends, may come :—
That heavenly home,—illimitable—free,
Oh, to be dwelling in its halls with thee !

MOTHERLESS.

I HAVE no mother !   O, ye ghostly winds
That wander in the gorges of the hills
As if ye sought and mourned for vanished friends,
Let me mourn with you !   Such a sorrow fills
My heart as never yet was known to yours ;
Though well the plaintive music of your voice
Accords with the sad wrecking of my joys,
And stricken Love that sorrows and endures.
What do you weep but smiling summers gone ?
Sweet blossoms withered that will blow again ?
But I am wounded in a vital part,
Smit through the heart's affections to the heart,
Which cries aloud for that belovéd one,
But all its calling is in vain, in vain !

THE SPELL BROKEN.

FAR from my native glen my years have flown :
    Only at intervals, or in my dreams,
    Have I revisited the pleasant streams
That strong affection bade me call my own.
Yet was I not unhappy, though the chill
    Of exile pain'd me ; many a happy thought—
    Many a message o'er the waters brought—
Told me I was a son of Wanlock still.
Now at one wrench the cherish'd tie is broken,
    The pleasing bondage ended ; I am free
    From all her spells save those of Memory—
(That ghost of dead things), and these give no token
That aught is left in hill or stream or plain
With power to draw me to their midst again.

OUR PORTION.

FATHERS will still toil here for those they love,
  Though ours be gone; mothers will watch and pray
  Though the belovéd voice be still'd for aye
That breath'd our names before the throne above.
Around bright hearths, as in old happy days,
  Dear friends, long parted, will be glad again;
But nevermore for us the kindly blaze
  Of Home will lighten Wanlock's lonely glen.
Less than the meanest flower beside the burn
  (That dies to bloom again) is there of place
  Or portion here for our far-scatter'd race;
No future Spring shall welcome our return:
Naught have we 'neath these skies that bend above
Save Memory—and the graves of those we love.

A SORROWFUL CHOICE.

RATHER than see a stranger in the seat
  Of my dear father, and irreverent hands
    Profane the things my sainted mother's touch
Made sacred (should my wandering feet
  Ever return from these far distant lands
    To that lost home I loved and honoured much),
Methinks it were a lesser pain to find
  The house in ruins ; all its old-time grace
  Utterly vanished—nor a lingering trace
Of what it had been, in the wreck behind.
More like my own sad heart that home would be
  Soulless and silent, dead to every tie ;
And the old hearth bereft of all its glee,
  Staring through naked rafters at the sky.

ON WANLOCK DOD.

(AFTER MANY YEARS.)

My foot is on my native heath ; my native air
 Blows freshly round me ; clear and sweet and strong
 The hill-bird sings his old familiar song,
And as of old the summer skies are fair.
Glad thoughts and proud my bosom oft have fill'd—
 Gazing upon this scene ; but Ah ! to-day,
 The saddest words that human lips could say
 Would little of the loneliness reveal
 That on this solitary watch I feel :
For all the voices that I lov'd are still'd ;—
 Gone are the dear ones that made Wanlock dear ;
A stranger stands within my Father's door :
 So changed it is, I will not venture near—
'Tis not the Wanlock that I lov'd of yore !

THE MYSTERY.

No place for me in Wanlock! Vacant chair
   At board or hearth await me there no more;
   Barring my entrance, the insensate door
That wont to welcome, opes not to my prayer.
Forth from this mystery I needs must fare,
   Seeking sweet solace, as I did of yore
   By whispering streamlet and on mountain hoar,—
But ah! no longer find I comfort there.
Calmly as ever on grey Auchenlone
   The gloaming falls; the dear familiar rills
As sweetly in the solitude sing on:
   But, dead to all the magic of the hills,
   In me no wakening chord responsive thrills
As in my native wilds I walk—alone!

CHANGED TIMES.

Time was when I could scarce restrain my pace
   Upon thy mountains, Wanlock; to and fro,
   From sheer delight, fleet as the bounding roe
My eager feet thy winding paths would trace.
Now with a sober and deliberate stride
   I move among them; calmer now the eye
   That notes the beauties of thy evening sky,
Tamer the glance that sweeps thy grey hillside.
Yet is it not advancing age alone
   That quells my ardour; far from thee and me
   All the associates in that early glee—
Father and mother, sister, friend—have gone;
And musing on the forms I meet no more
With slow sad steps I track thy mountains o'er.

TO A LAVEROCK

(SINGING IN THE CALM SHEUGH).

IF thy heart were as sad as mine, sweet bird,
  That sing'st in Wanlock like a thing inspired,
  Methinks thy tender breast could ne'er be fired
To pour such strains—the sweetest ever heard.
Ay, sweet indeed they are; and yet there seems
  A note of sadness in their keenest joy;
  Is thy bliss too, then, not without alloy?
Do ghosts of dear ones haunt thy songs and dreams?
Ah! 'tis the common lot; some day, some day,
Our heart's desire takes wings and flies away;
  We cannot keep our lov'd ones, and our strains
Are weak and broken when the hot tears fall;
  But this poor comfort at the worst remains—
'Tis well for us that we can sing at all.

TO REV. MR. BLAIR, WANLOCKHEAD.

Ev'n as a mist, that for a moment's space
   Enshrouds some mountain, and then trails away
   Leaving no token of that moment's stay,—
Nay, not a memory on the tranquil face,—
So I and mine from out our native place
   Have pass'd away for ever : short our day
   As the light mists that topp'd the mountain gray.
And leaving in our wake so little trace.
And yet perchance, some essence of that mist
   Trickling to earth in solitude unseen,
   Nourish'd a tiny plant and kept it green ;
   So would I, that remembrance of the days
We liv'd in Wanlock—though he scarcely wist—
   Might lead some friend to love our name always.

THE FLIGHT OF TIME.

How quickly do the hurrying years sweep by!
  It seems but yesterday that I was straying
  O'er heath-clad hills with boyish comrades playing,
My childhood's home and all its lov'd ones nigh.
Now these are gone ; that sweet home life is shatter'd,
  The home itself is home to me no more ;
'Neath many skies the friends of youth are scatter'd,
  And I, a wanderer on this distant shore,
O'er mine own brood with care and toil am rearing
  A sheltering rooftree ; but the same rude hand
  That broke my idols in the far-off land
This latest refuge of my years is nearing ;
A little while and that same brood will cry
And shudder in the night to see me die.

Poems and Songs.

MAY MORIL.

WE wonn'd in a lanesume muirlan' glen—
   May Moril and me,
And little we kent o' the ways o' men—
   May Moril and me ;
But if little we kent, far less did we care,
 Sae couthie and vaunty can true love be,
For we ettlet nae joy in the warld sae rare,
But micht ha'e been match'd in the muirlan' there,
When the glamour o' love fillt a' the air
 And we waded the brackens knee by knee.

Kings and their coorts micht founder or soom
   On their shiftin' sea ;
But we wi' their fate ne'er fasht oor thoom—
   May Moril and me.
We kent that the warld wad trintle and turn
 Wi' mickle o' pleasure and mair o' wae,
Sae doon by the banks o' the wimplin' burn
We strayed i' the dawin' o' love's sweet morn,
And we nippet the blossom and jinkt the thorn
 As the lang saft simmer row'd away.

9

The brier rose grew on the open shaw
     In the lown clear air,
And it and the milk-white blume o' the haw
     I twined in her hair :
And she sat on the brae like a gowd-croont queen
    And fliskit her sceptre o' birk wi' pride :
And I—I thocht that the joys we ken't
As lang as we socht them ne'er wad en't,
And e'en when oor hinmaist breath was spent
    We'd sleep i' the muirlan' side by side.

But alas ! for the unkent weirds o' man
     Are kittle tae dree,
And little we trow'd that oor gowden plan
     Sae brittle wad be.
But the heaven aboon us nae doot saw
    Our love was mair than it ocht tae be,
For we hadna been marriet a year and a day
When, sair forfeuchen, my winsome May
On the breist o' her dawtie dwined away,
    And my heart-strings crack't when I saw her dee.

O hooly and wae I laid her doun
     In her hinmaist rest,
And back i' the glen I lookit roun'
     At oor herrit nest :
And bare, bare noo were the muirlan's grey,
    Where the licht o' her love gart a' things shine,
And I saw that nocht i' the warld wad be
The same as it was tae my joyfu' ee,

When we wadit the brackens knee by knee,
And sweet May Moril was hale and mine.

The brier rose blumes on the open shaw,
As it did langsyne,
And the milk-white blossom hings on the haw
I' the warm sunshine.
But blossom and bud hae tint their charms,
They may rot where they gether or fa' for me,
And O ! gin I hadna a thocht tae rise
Tae sweet May Moril ayont the skies,
Where my heart baith e'enin' and mornin' lies,
Hoo sad wad the lang grey muirlan' be !

FORGOTTEN.

O BLESSINGS on thy bonnie face,
  My winsome Mary Lee !
And lang may fickle fortune trace
  A flowery path for thee.
May joy bring dimples roon thy mouth,
  Through a' the gowden years,
And never drink be near his drouth
  That weets thy cheek wi' tears !

I hae been fain tae win the smile
  That waukent in thine een,
And wrocht wi' mony a tentie wile
  Tae please thee morn and e'en ;
And though I didna daur to speak,
  My heart ne'er owned the fear
That thy young love wad ever seek
  Anither joe to cheer.

But now they say thou'rt woo'd and won,
  My winsome Mary Lee !
They tell me thou art woo'd and won,
  Withoot a thocht o' me ;

Withoot a memory o' the days
  My heart will never tyne,
When thou and I amang the braes
  Gaed linkin' blythe lang syne.

O Mary, could thy heart forget
  The kiss it yielded coy,
That nicht beside the plantin' yett,
  When I was gyte wi' joy?
Could it forget? or did it ken
  That mine thrill'd thro' and thro'?
Thou should hae kept thy favours then,
  Or no' withheld them noo!

That nicht I vowed a solemn aith,
  My winsome Mary Lee,
That nocht wad shake the simple faith
  I had in love and thee :
I pledged my soul upon the spot,
  Whatever fate micht fa' ;
But thou that gied, as sune forgot,
  And never lo'ed ava !

And still I dinna curse the day,
  When first thy face was seen ;
Though thou hast left me wauf and wae,
  I'm glad that day has been.
In memory's casket where each gem
  O' happiness is stored,
Nae days will ever match wi' them
  When thou wert maist adored.

Fareweel ! may gladness be thy lot,
   Without a grief to mar ;
A lanely wanderer clean forgot,
   I bless thee from afar :
And may thy lover ne'er hae cause
   A dule like mine tae dree—
Fareweel, I canna ca' thee fause !
   Forgetfu' Mary Lee !

ATWEEN AND MENNOCK-HASS.

Atween and Mennock-hass
   There is a cosy biel',
Whaur a bonnie lad and lass
   Micht haud a tryst fu' weel ;
And gin ye like, May Moril,
   As sune's the gloamin' fa's,
Ye're free tae share my plaidie there
   Frae every blast that blaws.

The muirlan' may be bare,
   And snell the norlan' breeze—
Little shelter rises there
   Save what yon craigie gies ;
But in my heart, May Moril,
   There is a blythesome glow,
And tae't sae fain I'll fauld your ain,
   That cauld ye'll never trow.

We'll hear the lintie sing
   His sang o' love and pride,
Blabbin', silly, thochtless thing,
   O' joys he canna hide.

But sweeter far, May Moril,
    And tae nae ear but thine,
I'll whisper lown, hoo ye hae stown,
    The heart that ance was mine.

I canna brag o' gear,
    Tae cleed and keep ye fine ;
Rough and raploch mountain cheer
    Maun please gin ye'll be mine.
But pree and pruve, May Moril,
    And think or ye decide ;
There's few sae fiel as them that biel'
    Ayont a shepherd's side.

THE DAYS OF OLD.

In the brave days of old, ere the falchion formed the
    plough,
  When courage steeled his sinew 'neath the banner and
    the brand ;
When the haughty crest of chivalry was free to every
    brow,
  And prowess was the test in every land :
O ! then the heart was chainless as the wind,—
  The mighty soul of Freedom scorned to pawn its pride
    for gold ;
And manliness and glory were the mottoes of the mind,
  In the brave days of old.

In that grand reign of right, never coward kept a crown.
  Nor cunning conquered valour with the supple guile
    of brain ;
For the iron heel of honour held the wily serpent down,
  And majesty was master in the main :
Then love and truth were foremost in the fight,—
  The smile of blushing beauty was the guerdon of the
    bold ;
And the victor's brow was laurell'd in his king and
    country's sight,
  In the brave days of old.

But that bright sun hath set, and the night that gathers
    round
  Is alive with all iniquities that batten in the gloom ;
And vainly does the poet seek to sanctify the ground
  With flowers that are but scattered o'er his tomb.
We hear no more the stirring trump and drum
    That cheer'd the eager warrior when the strife around
      him roll'd :
And the sweetest sounds that greet us are the memories
    that come
  From the brave days of old.

O ! would that we might wake, as from a hateful dream,
  To wed the noble purpose that our ancestors have
    shown ;
Our barks are ever drifting down upon a golden stream,—
  Wealth is the only standard that we own ;
For it we pledge the dearest hopes of life,—
    Brain and sinew, nay, the future of the soul is often
    sold :
And we seek it as the warrior sought his glory in the
    strife
  In the brave days of old.

THE CAIRN ON THE HILL.

Among the Lowther hills there is a grave,—
A cairn rough-shapen on the moorland lea—
And many a fond attempt I made to learn
To whose remains that mound a shelter gave,
And what of pride or strength might buried be,
Under the guardianship of such a cairn ;
But to no useful end,—it was a mystery
Unveiled in traditionary lore,
Passed over in the careless page of history,
Forgotten 'mong the glorious songs of yore ;
Yet on the fragrant heath I've often lain,
When the lone plover and the wild curlew
Startled the moorland with their mournful screams ;
Or, while the brooding gloom that wrapt the plain
Upon my soul its speechless glamour threw,
Sat pensively, and crooned my gloaming dreams.

I.

O thou in whom death's peaceful slumber
    Hath wrought the calm earth doth not know,
    Round whom no more the wave shall flow,
That wearies with its constant cumber
    All hearts that climb the climbing tide ;

What perfect rest is it that comes,
Unsought, and all life's ache benumbs,
Here where the wander'd wild-bee bums
    Along the mountain side.

II.

Not in the far heart of the city
    Broods such a silence as is here ;
    There sculptur'd towers and tombs appear,
To nourish love or waken pity
        With memories of the dust below :
        Forgetfulness of life is here,
        The very Lethe of the bier,
        And all along the moorland drear
            The dreary sense doth grow.

III.

Meet resting-place it is, though lonely,
    For mortal dead to name and fame ;
    And sure thine outlaw'd bones can claim
No righting at our hands, but only
        To lie where they have lain so long.
        If song or legend rung with praise
        Of thee, thine ashes we might raise,
        And honour yet ; but blame or praise
            Of thee is not in song.

IV.

The mountain peaks are bare and hoary
    That sentinel thy lonely grave :

No tree doth spring, no branches wave
To catch the burden of the story
    The breeze brings up the slumbering glen ;
And with its woful tale untold
The wind goes o'er the silent wold,
And all the secrets it doth hold
    Are lost to mortal ken.

v.

Perchance if on this naked mountain
    Some pine had stretch'd its arms abroad,
    And hawk or raven made abode
Within its crest, above the fountain
    That flows unshaded as we see,
At night the harping wind had stay'd
Amongst its boughs, and music made,
And to some gifted bard betray'd
    The secrets hid with thee.

vi.

But naught is known—the purple heather
    Is speechless in thy blame or praise ;
    The mourners who of old did raise
This cairn grown grey in wind and weather,
    Say neither thou wert base or brave,
Conjecture—rumour—all are mute,
Tradition—legend—know thee not,
These stones that mark the lonely spot
    But say— it is a grave.

VII.

Yet do I yearn to know thy station !
>Perhaps upon the scroll of fame
>Some kindly hand has traced thy name
A warrior in the Scottish nation
>>Whose actions show'd thee good and brave :
>If so—'tis meet that thou shouldst sleep,
>Among these mountains stern and steep
>That saw thy fatal broadsword sweep
>>Tyrants to a bloody grave.

VIII.

Perhaps thy lot was but the tending
>Of fleecy flocks upon these hills,
>Where the grey heath and noisy rills
Beneath a maze of mist are blending
>>Their features in the autumn gloam :
>Here while the summer hours flew by,
>Wrapt in thy chequered plaid to lie,
>And watch the clouds across the sky
>>Float on, like flakes of foam.

IX.

Or —higher thought—who knows but under
>These bleached stones the dust may rest
>That once was in the van to breast
The wave that dash'd itself in thunder
>>Against the rock of Scotland's faith ?

A martyr falling, book in hand,
When the rapacious Highland band
O'erran the vext unhappy land,
    And doom'd the good to death.

X.

Whate'er thou wert, forgotten sleeper,
    Will alter not thy deep repose ;
    Oblivion hides thy joys and woes,
And does not own a cavern deeper
        Than shrouds thy life from light and me ;
    For mists and mankind come and go,
    Midnight shapes flit to and fro,
    And, thinking not—unthought of—throw
        Shadows o'er thy grave and thee.

This is the meed the earth doth render
    To all except her brightest names ;
    A little while their merit claims
Her pride, that cherish and defend her,
        And then they're lost or toss'd away ;
    'Tis surely lesson this to me,
    From quest of earthly fame to flee,
    And rest my wishes where they'll be
        A treasure trove for aye.

RETROSPECT.

It's oh for a cot
  By the western main,
And a lowly lot
  To be mine again :
To feel as I felt
  When a dreaming boy,
And my fancy dwelt
  In the realms of joy.
When I knew no care,
  And I fear'd no foe,
Nor had thought to spare
  On a coming woe.
But morning and night
  Fresh pleasure would bring,
And my face was bright
  As a gladsome thing :
And a gladsome thing
  Of a truth was I
In that far-off spring
  That will never die !

I think of it now
  With an eye tear-wet,

The passionless brow
  And its crown of jet.
I think of it now
  With my locks grown white,
With a furrow'd brow
  And an eye's dim light.
I think of the change,
  So thorough and bold ;
Of the wider range
  In the thoughts I hold :
Of a life more known
  To my fellow-men
Than it could have grown
  In the narrow glen :
And well do I ween
  That the powers I hold
Would never have been
  In the life of old.

But balance the wealth
  Of a merchant proud
With the rosy health
  Of a boy snow-browed,
And up from the scales
  Is the red dust toss'd,
And its magic pales
  By the glory lost :
And fain would I give
  All my manhood's gains
For the spells that live
  In the bounding veins,

To revel once more
  In a region fair,
With power to explore,
  And spirit to share,
In signs that are rife
  In the earth and sea,
The mystery life
  Of the things that be.

What gladness it gave,
  In the rosy morn,
Afar on the wave
  To be lightly borne!
Blown out from the land
  On the sweet spring wind,
And leaving the grand
  Old mountains behind:
Away and away,
  Right out from the coast,
Till the hills grew grey
  And the glens were lost;
Till the full white sail
  Dropt empty and free
In the lessening gale
  Of the central sea:
And the trim wee bark,
  To the eagle's view,
Was the only mark
  In the world of blue.

Retrospect.

Sweet, too, the day long,
  My shallop to oar,
And listen the song
  Breathed round by the shore,
Where the long blue tide
  Rolls in from the sea
With its voice of pride
  And immensity :
Dim-telling of things
  In the far-off climes,
In music that rings
  Like a poet's rhymes.
And I listen'd, thrilled
  As the music grew,
Till my heart was filled
  With melody too ;
And that of the sea
  Seem'd kin to my own,
And stirr'd me with glee
  As I wander'd on—

Away 'mong the rocks,
  Where the eagle broods,
And the raven croaks
  To the summer floods :
Where the downy nest
  Of the eider-duck
Hangs high on the crest
  Of the sea-swept rock ;
And gulls on the beach
  Have their lowly home,

Scarce over the reach
　　Of the climbing foam.
Where never was heard
　　Since the world began,
A grovelling word
　　From the lips of man ;
For the wondrous gleam
　　That hallows the whole
Steals in like a dream
　　On the tranquil soul.

But more than the bliss
　　Of the morn or day
Was the stolen kiss
　　When the skies were grey ;
And the thrill—felt yet—
　　By the waterfall,
Where the two hearts met
　　That were all in all.
Come back to my heart
　　O days that are gone !
And bring me a part
　　Of the joy then known :
Come back, O ye days
　　Of gladness and mirth !
And light with your rays
　　My desolate hearth !
I'd barter a year
　　Of my after-gain
To breathe in the dear
　　Old boyhood again !

I PU'D A ROSE.

I PU'D a rose in Mennock wuds
   No lang sin', on my road gaun hame,
A mossy sprig wi' twa bit buds,
   Ye'd barely think deserved the name ;
But graff'd acqueesh a sproutin' tree,
   And eithly tentit e'en and morn,
As bonny a blossom opened e'e
   As ever busk't the laden thorn.

I woo'd a lass on Wanlock braes,
   A winsome birkie, bauld and slee ;
Whase life gaed by like summer days,
   Wi' lauch as licht and heart as free :
But sune the lowe that winna hide
   Gart Tibby's een grow wondrous fain,
And syne I saw wi' joyfu' pride
   Her heart was graffd acqueesh my ain.

GIN YE LO'E ME.

Gin ye lo'e me, lassie, meet me
   Up the Wanlock glen at e'en,
Where the wimplin' burnie wanders
   Through amang the knowes sae green ;
Where the bonnie bloomin' heather
   Sweetly scents the muirlan' air ;
I will tell ye o' a secret,
   Lassie, gin ye meet me there.

Ill wad set sae saft a story
   Tae be tauld in open day,
Wi' your thrawart minny glowrin'
   Owre ilk dawtie word I say ;
But when e'enin' cranreuch airts her
   Tae her couthie ingle-en',
Meet me, and I'll tell you something
   Some fowk wad be fain tae ken.

In the gloamin' glen the mavis
   Tells his mate how leal he lo'es ;
A' forenicht the hills o' Wanlock
   Hear how blythe the lintie woos ;
Ilka bird then nestles closely
   Tae some ither heart as kin',
But I'll never pree their gladness
   Till ye come and comfort mine.

THE LAST TOAST.

One more cup ere we rise from the board
  Where we sit in the daylight so dim,
Let the last ruddy drops of the vintage be poured,
  And bumper each bowl to the brim !
We drank to our Queen and our Fatherland too,
  While corks lay undrawn on our shelves ;
But this is the last, and give each one his due,
  Let the toast be this—to " Ourselves."

    Then, here's the last toast of the night,
      For we've drained every flask on the shelves,
    Get up, then, and drink it with meaning and might,
      And let the toast be—to " Ourselves."

England's Queen—we are proud, are we not,
  Of the deeds that ennoble this name ?
And we pray that the dastardly coward be shot
  That ever speaks light of her fame.
But Queens, at the best, are but seen from afar—
  Little more of this earth than the elves ;
Their glory comes to us like light from a star ;
  But we—we are facts to Ourselves.

    Then, here's the last, etc.

Scotland's hills of the heather and thyme
    Are dear to the hearts of the true,
And fondly we yearn in a far away clime
    To bring the wild peaks to our view ;
But chiefly they're dear from the worth of their sons—
    From the prince to the peasant that delves,
And how do we know but this quality runs
    In a trifling degree in—Ourselves ?

        Then, here's the last, etc.

MY AIN HILLS.

The bonnie hills o' Wanlock,
   I've spielt them ane and a',
Baith laich and heich and stey and dreich,
   In rain and rowk and snaw :
And owre a' ither mountains
   Nane else e'er bure the gree ;
Nae peaks that rise aneth the skies
   Can raise sic thochts in me.

I've warslet up Ben Lomond
   When simmer deckt its side,
And grey Goatfell, that stan's itsel'
   In solitary pride ;
But frae their wildest grandeur
   Wi' sma' concern I'd turn
Tae ae wee glen, wi' some I ken,
   By Wanlock's wimplin' burn.

For there wi' chiels far sunder'd,
   I roved in glee lang syne,
And never fit was lichter yet
   Amang the muirs than mine ;

And wi' sic shouts o' gladness
   We startlet hill and plain,—
I'd tyne a year o' a' things here
   Tae raise the like again.

But we are lads nae langer,
   And time is gowd they say ;
The hills sae green are seldom seen
   When ance we start tae stray ;
And mair than time is wantin',
   For gin we a' were there,—
Wha kens ? the min' micht no incline
   Its former sports tae share.

O, bonnie hills o' Wanlock !
   What pranks auld Time does play ?
I kent nae change in a' your range
   When I cam' here the day :
But faces that I met wi'
   . Are surely altert sair ;
And some I ken hae left the glen
   We'll never meet wi' mair.

But though the fit may wander,
   The heart can aye be true,
And mony a yin, I brawly ken,
   Wad fain be here e'enoo ;
And mony a weary comrade
   Like me fu' aften prays,
That the bonnie hills o' Wanlock
   May see his hinmaist days.

THE SEA.

BARDS sing the beauties of the deep,
 The ever-shifting wondrous main
Makes many a hand the harp-strings sweep,
 And lives in many a sounding strain,
But I, what beauty can I see
In that which parts my love and me?

I own its face may oft be fair,
 When summer skies are smiling o'er,
Or grand, when tempests gather there,
 And mad waves lash th' embattled shore,
But cannot view these sights with glee
The while it parts my love and me.

No other cause have I for hate,
 No friend of mine bemoans its power;
No hearts I loved have met their fate
 Upon it in the stormy hour;
Did it not part my love and me,
I too might sing the sounding sea.

But with such bar as this to break,
 How shall I teach my song to flow?

The only music I can make
   Dies in a dismal plaint of woe ;
I cannot bid that roll in glee
That rolls between my love and me.

And shall I therefore curse the deep ?
   Nay—for a whisper in mine ear
Makes all my pulses gladly leap,
   And tells me that the day is near
When o'er this wide mysterious sea
The waves will waft my love to me.

So, till that happy day shall dawn,
   Nor blame nor praise have I for thee,
Weird waste, whose witchery has drawn
   Music from every bard but me ;
But safely guide her bark along,
And I will thank thee in a song.

IN THE FOREST.

WHEN the red leaves fell on every side,
  And the straggling boughs were nearly bare,
I wander'd far through the forest wide,
  In the settled calm of the evening air.

The strong, fierce heat of the day was gone,
  The light winds folded their wings in rest,
And softly the streamlet murmur'd on
  With a childlike joy to the open west.

I follow'd the stream, for my heart inclin'd
  To list its tale to the witching close ;
And peace grew up in my musing mind
  As the gurgling melody wan'd and rose.

How sweet, I thought, to be always here,
  Away from the garish, noisy day ;
And my life to glide like the streamlet clear
  In the thrall of the flowery forest brae.

No chafing with rocks, no surging foam ;
  Naught but the flowers, the buds, and me ;
And the only change when I sought my home,
  As the stream must do, in the parent sea.

And even at last my spirit would crave
　　No boon that Nature is scant of here,
For the birds might mould me a leafy grave,
　　And whistle a dirge at my lonely bier.

But lo! as I plann'd in a blind content,
　　With never a thought beyond the trees,
To the edge of the forest my footsteps bent,
　　Led on by the rush of the nearing seas ;

And right through the struggling arms of pine
　　The broad, red sunset smote my brow ;
And I halted, abash'd, in the light divine
　　While the old dream fell like a leaf from the bough.

For I saw, what erst I had fail'd to see,
　　In the depths of the forest's rayless gloom,
That the stream might end in the parent sea,
　　But not my soul in the sealike tomb.

" And yonder," I cried, " is the goal for me !
　　The depths of the forest may suit the stream,
But I, with a future over the sea,
　　Have more to do than be here and dream."

CARRON WATER.

BONNILIE blinks the moon on Carron—
　Wimplin' awa,
Doon frae the hichts sae stey and barren,
Worn, wi' the rocks in the lang linns warrin',
　Sleepily slidin' by hamlet and ha',
　　Through the woodlan's free;
　O, bonnilie blinks the mune owre't a'!
But never a blink that she cuist on Carron
　Could equal in witchery them that fa'
　　Frae my winsome May on me.

Merrily lilt the birds on Carron,
　Deavin' the glen!
Nae note o' the lark's wi' the linty's jarrin'—
Nor the merle the mellow-tuned mavis marrin'—
　A' like a dream to the raptur'd ken
　　As the lays are sung;
　O, merrily lilt the birds ilk yin!
But never a sang that they sung on Carron
　Was half sae sweet as the words that rin,
　　Like hinny, frae my love's tongue.

Sweetly the wild flowers bloom on Carron,
 Buskin' the brae;
Blue-bell and primrose the greenwood starrin'—
Wild briar, rich as the roses o' Sharon—
 Violets and pinks frae ilk woodland way
  Fling balm on the gale;
  O, sweetly they bloom through the lang summer
   day!
But the sweetest flow'r on the banks o' Carron
 Is my rose-lipp'd, hazel-eyed, lily-brow'd May,
  The pride o' her native vale.

Dear to my heart are the links o' Carron;
 But far mair dear
Than the richest floweret the greenwood starrin',
Or the bonniest blink o' the mune on Carron,
 My May, wi' a voice as saft and clear
  As the wild bird's tongue;
  O, what do I care ocht else to hear!
Her love is mair to my heart than Carron,
 And weel do I trow that voice mair dear
  Than the sweetest sang e'er sung!

GLENBALLANTYNE ; OR, MY LAST LOOK O' HAME.

I HAE wander'd far i' the wilds this day,
  Owre heichts bent-clad, and in howes sae green ;
I hae heard weird words that I daurna say,
  And sichts that were not o' the yird I've seen.

And sair I misdoot I hae lookit my last
  On bonnie green howm and on brairdit lea,
For a freit, like a chirt o' the norlan' blast,
  Lies cauld, lies cauld at the heart o' me.

O, licht is the fitstep, leisomely fain,
  Tho' weary wi' raikin' and stiff wi' toil,
That the gloamin' o' life brings back again
  To the kindly touch o' its native soil !

To spiel ance mair the stey green hills
  Sae lichtly esteem'd when the heart was high,
And dauner again by the wimplin' rills
  That croon sae sweet o' the days gane by.

Cauld maun the heart be, twin'd o' its joys,
  And weary the weird that heart maun dree
That comes to the scenes o' its youthfu' ploys
  Wi' never a spark o' its youthfu' glee.

11

For me—the blude i' my bosom lap
  Wi' a schule-bairn's joy turn'd lowse to play
When I lookit again on the lane hill tap,
  And the glen where I spent life's early day.

And never sae fair did the auld hills seem
  I' the years langsyne as they did this day,
When I cross't at the heid o' the Wanlock stream,
  Wi' the bird i' the lift, and the blume on the brae.

I hadna been gane on the muirs a mile,
  A mile on the muirs, but barely twa,
When the sun o' the simmer ceas'd to smile,
  And the sweet hill win' it was airtit awa':

And a'thing grew sae eerie and lown
  By Enterkin-Hass and the Lowther Brae,
I made for the heichts, as I wad hae flown,
  For laich i' the glens I couldna stay.

I hadna been oot on the heichts a mile,
  A mile on the heights, but only three,
When a mist row'd doon on the braid Steygyle,
  And happit his buirdly bouk frae me.

Sae wan were its faulds, sae dern and wan,
  'Twas mair like a flowther o' drivin' snaw,
And I neither could see where the burnie ran,
  Nor catch ae note o' its lilt ava'.

And in the glenheid, or ever I wist,
  Where the lang witch-bracken is stiff and still,
I yokit wi' them I wad fain hae miss't—
  The dreid white faces that haunt the hill.

For, richt i' my gate, a' waesome and worn,
  The yirdit deid, whase name I beir,
Were waitin' for me, by the muirlan' burn—
  An awsome trystin' o' dule an' fear.

The dear deid faces—the lips I've kiss't—
  The een that langsyne look't luve i' my ain—
They gapit and glowre't frae the muirlan' mist,
  And they fley'd me, and into the mist again :

And up on the heichts I could hear their cries ;
  I can hear them yet ! I sall never tine
The gruesome dreid at my heart that lies
  Sin' the sauls o' my kinsfolk spak' wi' mine !

Ye may busk i' yer brawest, Glenballantyne burn
  (And o' lown sweet beauty ye hae your share) ;
But a' my thochts frae your memories turn,
  And I'll taigle at e'en i' your neuks nae mair.

Farewell, green Lowther—corrie and brae !
  A lang fareweel ye may tak' o' me ;
I hae hauden a tryst i' your wilds this day,
  That'll keep me fey till the day I dee.

AMANG THE BRUME.

Doon amang the brume, in yon dowie glen yestreen,
　I heard a safter melody than mavis ever sang;
And I couldna fen' but listen tho' a mist cam' in my een,
　And ilka word gaed through me like a stang—
"O bonnie rides the boat when the simmer win' is lown,
　And the gowden lift abune her is nae sooner than the
　　sea;
But when the win' is waken't, and the wave has gurly
　　grown,
　What troubles maun the weary boatie dree!"

Doon amang the brume, when the eerie wail gaed by,
　A dwawm cam' owre my kennin', and I saw a boat
　　gaun doon;
And I wist the warst had happen'd, for I heard a waefu'
　　cry,
　And again the voice gaed through me wi' a stoun—
"O! bonnie is the lift when the storm has cleart the
　　blue,
　And bonnie is the water when it settles braid and fair;
But the bonnie face o' somebody will smile nae mair on
　　you,
　His boat will ride the waters nevermair."

THE POET AND HIS THEME.

FOREVER o'er the sea of song
 The poet's fairy shallop glides ;
In mirth and music borne along,
 It lightly breasts the bounding tides.

From morn till night awake, asleep,
 He threads the bay, or skirts the shore ;
The rolling numbers of the deep
 Are in his heart for evermore.

No stormy gust invades the calm
 That broods between his sea and sky ;
But silent, low, and rich with balm
 The slumbrous zephyr wanders by.

He lives in love with all around ;
 He changes as the seasons fill ;
His heart—a lyre of sweetest sound—
 Is strung and swept by Nature still.

The memories of the olden time
 Are wafted to him down the wind ;
He knows the songs of every clime,
 And sets them to each mood of mind.

And when the night is near at hand
 He cons them over one by one ;
And far across the listening land
 The magic of his lay is blown.

He sings of life, and love, and death,
 Of all things bright and fair to see ;
And in the pauses of his breath
 The waves complete the melody.

But, most of all, he loves the theme
 Of years to come when sin is dead ;
Then rolls his music in a stream
 Impassioned, chaining heart and head.

For, more than all things great or dear
 The ages leave us as they roll,
This longing for the golden year
 Is centred in the poet's soul.

Oh, gentle bard, that longs to greet
 The day when all hearts throb like thine !
How many weary years must fleet
 Across the land in storm and shine ?

How many loves that now are bright
 Will darken into worse than scorn
Before we burst this dismal night
 That drags us from the golden morn ?

So deep the shade on hut and hall,
   So seldom glints the fitful gleam,
Alas ! I fear that, after all,
   It lives but in the poet's dream !

AT THE GARDEN GATE.

THE moon, like a shepherdess, climbs the steeps
  Where her silent flocks of stars are straying,
And lightly down through the dark blue deeps
  Her cloudy robes on the breeze are playing :
The spell of the night is on mountain and main,
  Woodlands and waters are swathed in sleep ;
And fitful and faint on the night wind's wings
Is wafted the dirge that the streamlet sings,
  As it glides through the glen to its grave in the deep.

Alone by the garden gate as I stand,
  I think of a night—just such another—
When I waited here to touch the hand
  Dear to me yet above all other :
Just so—did the moonlight tip the trees ;
  Just so—the night wind rose and fell ;—
Ah me! how long should I linger now,
With the night-wind stealing across my brow,
  Ere the touch of that hand would break the spell

WALLACE.

On the page of Scottish story,
  Red with valour though it be,
Who can lay such claim to glory
  As the knight of Elderslie?
Wallace, first of all the warriors
  Ever belted blade on thigh,
May the heart that slights thy greatness
  Droop in dungeon dark and die!

Bruce was wise, and Douglas daring;
  Randolph's heart was stout and bold;
Stern Kirkpatrick's sword unsparing;
  Fraser loved by young and old:
But in thee alone, proud Wallace,
  Burn'd the quenchless patriot flame:
All the rest had stooped to England,
  Borne awhile a traitor's shame.

Well their after-deeds absolved them
  From the stain that dimm'd their shield,
And when England's king resolved him
  They should die or meanly yield,

O how leapt each manly bosom,
　Thrill'd by Bruce's gathering cry,
And beneath his glorious banner
　Took the field to do or die.

But in thee no stain existed,
　Oath of thine no king could claim ;
Evermore thy sword resisted
　All that spoke in Edward's name.
How could then the doom of traitor
　Be assigned with truth to thee,
When thy soul disdained to own him
　For a king—in chains or free ?

But the fools who deem'd thee traitor
　Knew not then as we know now,
That thy death has made thee greater,
　Wreath'd fresh laurels round thy brow :
For although to live a patriot
　Tries the strength of heart and will,
He who dies a patriot-martyr
　Proves devotion deeper still.

Spotless as the vault of heaven
　Was thy soul's untainted glow ;
And to such alone is given
　Power to check the tyrant foe :
Down through all the after ages
　Beams that radiance full and clear,—
Who shall say it doth not reach us,
　Seated in our freedom here ?

PAIRING-TIME.

I HEARD the muirhens in the dawin',
　　And siccan a rippet they raised!
Sae crousely the muircocks were crawin',
　　I glowert as the birds had been crazed;
For I thocht that the hamely employment
　　O' biggin' a nest had been quiet;
But gin it can yield sic enjoyment,
　　What say ye, young lassie, to try't?

The muircock is blithe wi' his dearie,
　　A' nicht in the howe o' the hill;
But lang were the gloamin' and eerie,
　　If spent on the muir by himsel':
And what is a man withoot woman,
　　But a muircock that hasna a hen?
Sae bide wi' me noo in the gloamin',
　　And shorten my nicht in the glen.

A cozy wee cot and a cannie,
　　Is ready whenever ye will,
Weel plenished wi' plenishin' bonnie,
　　And wantin' for nocht but yoursel':
Then come in the gloamin', my treasure!
　　For troth I am weary tae ken,
Gin pairin'-time brings the birds pleasure,
　　What wonderfu' joys it gies men.

THE DEATH-SONG OF TIME.

In the empty years that loom upon the world
   Ere the mountains shall be levell'd with the sea,
Or the blackening bolt of thunder shall be hurled
   From the caverns of the life that is to be,
Mute and haggard on the margin of his power,
   'Mong the nations that are crumbling in his shade,
Robed in all the passing splendour of the hour,
   Time is leaning like a warrior on his blade ;
And he feels the sickly flaring of the sun,
   Hears the slogan of the breeze that rushes past,
And marks the ebbing ages as they run
   Among his fingers, wearing quickly to the last ;
Then, rising to the fulness of his form,
   He passionately clamours to the throng,
And louder than the roarings of the storm
   Comes the music of the mighty wizard's song :—

" Get ye hence and be forgotten !   Who are ye
   Clinging wonder-stricken round the skirts of Time ?
Have ye left your homes in idleness to see
   The shadow that will blast ye in your prime ?

Do ye think the lion leaves his cave to die,
 That the meaner beasts may triumph in his pain ?
Though the light be fading surely from mine eye,
 It will burn till yours can never glint again !

" Mine arm hath been against ye all my days,
 I have conquer'd and will conquer to the end ;
There is no mortal force that ye can raise
 But the iron guard of Time will turn and bend.
Ye are not what ye were no more than I,
 I have worn away your nerve and sapp'd your will ;
It is not long to linger—surely I
 That have borne so long can bear a little still.

" O the tooth of dull decay hath toucht the hills,
 And soon their flaunted pride will be no more,
And wearily the wrinkled ocean spills
 The weepings of his dotage on the shore ;
All things which were of old are waxing grey,
 And if such things as these can cease to be,
What hope have ye, the insects of a day,
 To wrestle through this weary war with me ?

" It is not many days that I must wait
 Till the fulness of your time be come and gone,
I will leave ye, drawn together, to your fate,
 And the spell will settle o'er ye one by one.
Man and matron, prince and peasant, young and old,
 The coward's dust shall mingle with the brave ;
Many flocks are penn'd together in a fold
 When the world is not a dwelling but a grave.

" And when ye walk no more upon the earth,
 And your feet have left no traces where they trod,
When the stately halls that echoed with your mirth
 Are not left to tell the future your abode ;
When the very name of man has been forgot,
 And all the fierce emotions of his prime,
The longings and the labours of his lot
 Are like mists upon the memory of Time ;

" When the mountain and the meadow shall be one,
 And the glamour of the glen hath ceas'd to be ;
When the mystery of the midnight and the moon
 Cannot rouse the slumbering madness of the sea ;
When the sun that shines so feebly shines no more,
 And the primal darkness settles o'er the deep,
I will push my silent shallop from the shore,
 Glide away into Eternity—and sleep ! "

EL DORADO.

WHERE is the land of the sunlight and shadow,
  Rivers of silver and mountains of gold ;
The beautiful province yclept El Dorado,
  Imaged erewhile by the dreamers of old?
Seek it no more where the sounding Atlantic
  Murmurs its mystical tales in your ear ;
Come, I will show you the region romantic !
  Listen, the true El Dorado is here.
      A silent wind from a far blue sky,
        A bark on the lake in the clear moonshine,
      The first look of love in a merry blue eye,
        And a dear little hand in mine.

Say not 'tis false that the country we live in,
  Old mother England, the free, may contain
The peace and the plenty for which ye have striven,
  Deeming them far in the orient main ;
Back from the lands of the sun to our valleys !
  This is the haven to which ye should steer ;
The light and the gloom of the magical palace—
  Treasures uncounted and countless are here :—
      A silent wind from a far blue sky,
        A bark on the lake in the clear moonshine,
      The first look of love in a merry blue eye,
        And a dear little hand in mine.

Love is the " sesame " that opens our nature,
 Gifting our vision with power to behold
The fair face of earth, with a smile on each feature,
 Making it truly a region of gold.
Come, then, ye hearts that with longing are weary,
 Think not the world is faded and sere,
Much that we know may be gloomy and dreary,
 But surely the true El Dorado is here :—
  A silent wind from a far blue sky,
   A bark on the lake in the clear moonshine,
  The first look of love in a merry blue eye,
   And a dear little hand in mine.

ENTERKIN.

THERE'S a glen, i' the far-aff hills o' my hame,
  I'll ne'er forget ;
A glen wi' a sweet auld-farrant name
  That thrills me yet ;
Thrills me, and fills me wi' nameless joy
As the sicht o't did when a dreamin' boy,
And I lay at e'en on the grey hillside,
My young heart loupin' wi' stouns o' pride
At thocht o' the ferlies ye hae seen,
Warrior and martyr, lover and freen—
A' tint noo to the hill folk's e'en !
 Oh, Enterkin ! I hae wander't far
Owre land and sea ;
 But sweetest o' a' sweet memories are
My dreams o' thee !

Then streikit at ease on the lane glenheid,
  Oor cracks wad be
O' the dauntless word and the baulder deed
  That set men free ;
Free to meet i' the wilds and pray
To God, i' their ain sweet simple way.
Peacefu' and happy is Enterkin—
A lowner glen ye wad hardly fin' :

A'body comes and gangs at will,
Safe as the sunlicht on the hill—
Never a heart taks tent o' ill.

  Oh, weel may the auld days fill wi' thocht
Ilk pensive min',
  For the freedom and safety there were bocht
Wi' blude, langsyne !

For there, i' the gowden youthfu' days
     O' love and pride,
When a Sabbath calm had husht the braes
     At gloamin' tide :
The forms that I loe'd best to see
Were wont to dauner at e'en wi' me ;
The kindly auld folks led the way,
But watcht that we didna jouk or play ;
Sister and brither, and comrade dear,
And aiblins a sweet young stranger here,
Borrow'd frae Lunnon ance a year :
  Oh, blaw thou saft in her bonnie face,
Thou westlin' win' !
  For a winsomer sicht did never grace
Grey Enterkin !

Though lanesome and laich be the soun's that creep
     Through Enterkin,
Nocht waur than the bleat o' the wild hill sheep
     Disturbs the glen,
The sugh o' the win', the burnie's moan,
Or the cry o' the whaup on Auchenlone ;

Enterkin.

Little ye'd dream o' the fearsome day
When the red-coats fill'd yon narrow way
Where the men o' the Covenant took their stand
For the martyr-faith o' their native land,
And stern MacMichael led the band :
   Oh, sweet be his slumber in auld Kirkbride,
That warrior grim ;
   For the feck o' the charm o' yon grey hillside
Was wrocht by him !

Oh, bonnily there on the muirlan' heicht
     The sun looks doon,
And bauldly up i' the warm sunlicht
     Ilk hauds his croon :
Lowther and Steygyle, Auchenlone—
Daintiest hill that the licht looks on :
(Aft hae I spiel'd its benty side
Wi' freens noo sinder'd far and wide),
While bonnily owre baith burn and brae
The sklentin' shadows o' e'enin' play,
And syne hap a' at the close o' day :
   Oh, surely the weird, uncanny skill
O' elfin' wand
   Ne'er cuist mair glamour on howe and hill
In fairy-land !

Oh, saftly blaw, thou win' o' the west
     Through Enterkin !
And shine oot, Sun, in thy splendour drest,
     On Enterkin !

A' things bonnie and heartsome be
Aye like a halo o' peace roon thee :
And i' the hearts o' warldly men
That come to look on this lanesome glen,
Peace, like the peace that slumbers there—
Peace, like the peace that follows prayer,
Fa', like the dewdraps, unaware !

    Oh, fain wad I niffer a towmond's joy
This side the sea

    To feel as I felt when a dreamin' boy
Langsyne in thee !

THE CRY OF THE HILLMEN.

God o' the Hameless, shield Thy bairns !
   Loutt laich frae oot Thy halie hauld,
And i' the bield o' Thy wicht airms
   This remnant o' Thy flock enfauld ;
Else ane by ane we'll dwine awa'
   Like lilts o' sang-birds frae the hill,
When e'ening mirk begins to fa',
   And gleds and hoolits work their will.

For never did the lintie's heid
   Clap closer to the bien hillside
While owre her swept that form o' dreid,
   Than God's ain folk are fain to hide ;
A' day we shun the licht ; at e'en
   We seek the dusht and darksome glen,
Weel, if the midnicht's murky screen
   But hap us frae oor fellow men !

Here, stowlins, amang craigs and howes,
   In cauld and weet, we're forced to bide ;
Oor only feres the tods and yowes
   That raik alang the mountain side ;

The wild bird's wheeple frae the lift
　　The only leevin' voice we hear,
Save when in some lane glen we lift
　　Oor ain to Thee in dule and fear.

Nocht ken we o' the joys of life,
　　The ingle-neuk, the heartsome ha',
Oor bonnie bairns and blithe gudewife,
　　For Thy sake, Lord! we've tint them a';
Yet wad we coont oor losses, gains,
　　Gin Thou in mids' o' us wad be
To ease us o' the skaith and pains
　　That we maun for oor Covenant dree.

It's oh that we micht bauldly stan'
　　In Christ's ain kirk amang oor kin,
Thy halie Book in ilka han',
　　Thy praise ilk gledsome saul within;
For this oor Covenant we mak',
　　For this we thole, for this we dee;
Oor han's are on the pleugh, and back
　　Ae wistfu' glance we maunna gie.

Hoo lang, oh Lord! wilt Thou abide
　　In Thy heich-hadden withoot sign,
While ravenin' wolves on ilka side
　　Herry and rive this fauld o' Thine?
The bluid o' mony a martyr'd saint
　　Cries to Thee frae the muirlan' sod;
Oh, loutt and listen to oor plaint,
　　Bare Thy wicht airm and bield us, God!

HAME'S AYE HAME.

(THE LINTIE'S DEFENCE OF THE MOORLAND.)

" BONNIE wee bird wi' the blithesome e'e,
  Happin' aboot on the bare hillside,
Liltin' yer sang wi' a heart as free
  As the breeze that scatters it far and wide.
What can hae ta'en ye—if I may spier—
That ye suld bide i' the muirlan' here?"

" What can hae ta'en me? Whaur wad I gang
  Tae look for a joy I lack e'enoo?
Is there a spot thir hills amang
  Wi' heather as bonnie or lift as blue?
Tell me the marrow o' Arthur's Grain,
This lane lown corrie I ca' my ain."

" Arthur's Grain is but scraggy and bare,
  Hardly a bracken tae bield ye here;
Mennock has wudlan's bonnie and fair
  Whaur ye micht shelter the leelang year,
And join wi' the lave o' the feather'd thrang,
Deavin' the wuds wi' yer joyfu' sang."

" Mennock is bonnie, and fair, and fine,
  But mony a blither than me is there :
And wha wad listen tae sangs like mine
  When the wuds are ringin' wi' soons sae rare ?
On the bleak, bare muir, or the misty glen
Ye bless the voice ye wad ne'er hear then."

" But gleds come whiskin' athort the muir,
  Yer wee heart loups tae yer neb wi' dreid ;
Ye ken thae brackens are no secure,
  Ilk wauf o' the win' micht shaw yer heid ;
And what wad become o' yer artless glee
Gin ye catcht the tail o' his ruthless e'e ? "

" The gleds come roun' by the muir, as ye say,
  And oh, but their glance is gleg and keen ;
But better a gled in the open day
  Than a hoolit's skraich i' the mirksome e'en ;
When the heart's warm bluid begins tae creep
Wi' an eerie chill, and ye daurna sleep."

" But think o' the storms ye maun endure,
  And the faucht ye hae for a pyke betimes.
It's hard, dry fare on a barren muir,
  And little ye get for yer winsome rhymes ;
And sangs come best frae a singer's heid
That ne'er maun think on claes or breid."

" Storms at the warst maun e'en blaw by,
  And the young ling blumes are sweet tae pree ;

And then sae fair is the simmer sky,
    Ye'd sing for pleasure as weel as me.
Claes, I'll be thankfu', come aff haun,
And a gey wee mouthfu' keeps me gaun."

" Aweel, wee bird, I hae said my say,
    Ye may bide i' the cauld, bare muir for me ;
Ne'er think I'd be fain tae see ye away,
    'Twas a' for yersel' I made sae free.
The muir wad be dowie and deid I troo
Gin it hadna a leevin' voice in you."

" Nae mair ; gin the voice o' the muir be sweet,
    Still let it be as it aye has been ;
In simmer or winter, cauld or weet,
    The hills are dear to my constant een :
For wi' birds, as wi' mair things I could name,
Nae maitter hoo lowly—hame's aye hame."

LITTLE THINGS.

Long have I revelled in the book of nature,
  Those wondrous pages that were penned of old,—
And sought to fathom in each varying feature
  The mystic lore its hieroglyphics hold:
And more convinced am I the more I ponder,
  That lessons meant for us are seldom found,
While we sit tranced in a grateful wonder
  To see the everlasting wheel go round.
Though not with soul quite dead to all the glory
  That breathes around us in the open day,
'Tis but the main points of the sounding story
  We catch, blown down upon our dusty way.
The grand old hills that rear their crests to heaven,
  The stately streams that ever seek the sea,
The deep ravines with echoing thunder riven,
  The golden glory of the harvest lea,—
These all men know: but few without emotion,
  Alone within the mellow eventide,
Could pace the limit of the sounding ocean,
  Or rest upon the silent mountain side.
But though we note the lesson thrust before us
  In the long biding awe such presence brings,
We mostly fail to catch the joyous chorus
  Rung ever in our ear by lesser things.

The little flower that blooms beside the highway,
   The little brook that wimples through the glen,
The little bird that sings in every bye-way,—
   All have their little tale for heedful men.
They are the gentlest outcomings, the feelings
   With which great Nature's heart doth overflow ;
They touch our sense with plaintive fond appealings
   At every corner, as we come and go.
They are the antidotes to all our fretting
   And paltry little cares of every day,
And in the heart, past chance of all forgetting,
   Memory should treasure every word they say.

LIKE THE RIVER.

O THE glad voice of the river
  Flings its music round and round,
And the glen is filled for ever
  With the waters' pleasant sound ;
But by neither wood nor meadow
  Will the rolling river bide—
Never rest in shine or shadow
  Till it reach the ocean wide.

And not surer does the fountain
  Send its waters to the sea,
From beyond the distant mountain,
  Than my heart its thoughts to thee.
Other eyes may catch unwitting
  Fitful glimpses here and there,
But to thine alone, love-litten,
  Is my inmost bosom bare.

Far among the upland hollows,
  When the gladsome stream was young.
Brighter flowers adorned the valleys,
  Louder mirth around it rung.

But through all their pride the river
  Lightly wandered fancy free,
Till it found its home for ever
  In the bosom of the sea.

So, in youth, I made each pleasure
  For a while my guiding star ;
Sought it, as they seek for treasure,
  Late and early, near and far ;
Till the silver starlets perished
  On the pallid marge of day,
And the hopes so fondly cherished,
  Like the stars had passed away.

Then I came, as comes the river,
  Leaving all the past behind ;
All the toil and the endeavour
  Of the restless youthful mind.
And with calmer voice and feeling,
  Here beside the peaceful sea,
To thy tender heart appealing,
  Left my happiness with thee.

ONLY A DREAM.

I DREAMT that the veil was drawn
  That screens the coming days,
And all the future folded there,
In the book of mystery laid bare,
  Before my wilder'd gaze.

And methought I seized the book,
  And read it page by page,
And I saw that life for me was still
A weary climb on a pathless hill,
  From youth till doting age.

There was no poet's wreath
  To ring my throbbing brow,
No sacred calm when the din was by,
Nor light to hallow the even' sky—
  All dreary then as now.

And I thought if this be truth,
  And the end is as I see,
'Tis surely a wilful waste of time
Striving to reach that radiant clime,
  Whose sweets are not for me.

Then I woke—and lo ! the dream
   Fell from me as the snow
Falls from the branch in the early morn,
When the first keen glance of the sun has worn
   Its hold, and it slips below.

And as the branch breaks out
   And buds in the open day,
A nobler thought possessed my soul,
When the searching light of the sun did roll
   My snow-like dream away.

For I knew that the thing I saw
   Was born of the restless brain,
And not God-sent to bear me back,
With a sense of the many gifts I lack,
   Ere I a goal might gain.

So I work with earnest will,
   And a heart that still hopes on ;
And if no crowning wreath appears
At least I know in the rolling years
   Some faithful work is done.

THE BURN'S ANSWER.

BONNIE burn, that rins
  Tae the roarin' sea,
Hae ye no a word ava
  Frae the hills tae me?

Ye row'd by a shiel,
  In a far-aff glen,
Whaur a bonnie lassie bides
  That we baith suld ken.

For aft hae we roved
  By your bosky braes;
Ye tentit a' oor love dream,
  Its joys and its waes.

That gowd glint o' heaven
  Ye never wad forget.
O, tell me, bonnie burnie,
  Is her heart mine yet?

The bonnie burn grat.
  "O, bairn! I wad fain
Bring the news that ye spier for,
  To cheer ye again:

" That shiel in the glen
   Still stan's by my side,
And the lang and bosky howms
   In their simmer pride ;

" But the lass—wae's me !—
   She's a wife lang syne,
And the gowd dream has faded
   In your heart and mine ;

" There's nocht yonder noo
   Brings gladness tae me,
And I'm fain tae hurry by
   Tae the roarin' sea."

SCOTLAND'S CHARMS.

O LIGHTLY laughs the sailor lad
  That knows my pride and me,
And straight he speaks of wondrous lands
  Beyond the sounding sea ;
But never a tale I've heard him tell
  Could force my heart to own,
There ever were hills like Scotland's hills,
  Where Freedom has fixed her throne.
     Then here's to the hills of Scotland,
      Where the heather is waving free,
     There are no hills like Scotland's hills,
      Nor any so dear to me !

O proudly boasts the soldier bold,
  Who shows a victor's scars,
That none can match the dauntless foes
  He faced in foreign wars ;
But something more than a soldier's boast
  Should force my heart to yield,
There ever were men like Scotland's men
  Drawn up on a tented field.
     Then here's to the men of Scotland,
      Wheresoever their footsteps stray,
     There are no men like Scotland's men,
      No nation so bold as they !

O softly sighs the gallant gay,
  For some dark beauty's smile,
Whose charms still keep his fancy fixed
  On her lone flowery isle;
But say, shall an idle gallant's flame
  Have power to make us know
There ever were maids like Scotland's maids,
  As far as the winds can blow?
    Then here's to the maids of Scotland,
      With their eyes of the heaven's own blue,
    There are no maids like Scotland's maids,
      No hearts that are half so true!

SOMETHING WRANG.

I.

SAFT is the note o' the roguish bird that sits in the
flowery thorn,
When he woos some jaud frae the necbor shaw tae lie
a' nicht at his side ;
Blithe is the blink o' his gleg wee ee when it opes in the
mirk o' the morn,
And sees the dear thing cuddlet sae close he canna
but chirrup for pride.
But never did lovesick bird on the bough e'er pipe sae
sweet for a mate,
Never sic joy in a feathered breast has been sin' the
warld begun,
As I saw unseen when my winsome wife cam' oot tae
the door and flate,
That Willie suld leave her a day for the waters, Willie,
her favourite son.

II.

" Gie me your rod," quo she, "and bide ye at hame, I
hae muckle tae say ;
Ye come like a glouf o' the winter sun, yin hardly
kens ye are here,

Till the wee short fortnicht has worn tae an end, and
  then ye're aff and away ;
  And we seena the glisk o' your bonnie face maybe for
    anither year ;
Forbye ye ken o' the tryst I made wi' the neebors up by
  in the glen,
  That sax in the e'enin' wad bring them your faither,
    and me, and yoursel' ;
It never wad dae tae begunk them noo, especial, for
  weel ye maun ken,
  That the wish o' my heart and your faither's is bent
    on your matin' wi' Nell.

III.

"She's a trig lass Nell, and a bonnie, her marrows are
  no tae be fun'
  For parishes roun' though mony are in them bonnie
    and braw !
At this the rogue leuch till I thocht he wad fa'n tae the
  grun',
  And cryin' oot, 'Mither, that's gospel,' he hirselt
    aboot tae gae wa' ;
She, shakin' her nieve at the laddie, ance mair bade him
  think on the time,
  And then stood watchin' his buirdly make as he
    snoov'd in the dawin' alang,
Till he cam' tae the neuk where the fitroad dips, and he
  took tae the heather tae climb,
  When he turnt for a moment and shouted, 'I'll be, if
    there's naething gaes wrang.'"

IV.

Back tae the cottage she turnt her aboot, wi' the licht o'
    her love in her ee,
    And I met her fair i' the teeth and spier'd gin the tryst
        she made wad be held ;
And she, yet warm wi' her darlin's words, in simple and
    mitherly glee,
    Gade by wi' an answer that left me wauf, like a
        staggerin' stirk half-fell'd ;
For whether it was that the voice unkent had something
    o' dreid in itsel',
    Or whether my heart got a haud o' the words, like the
        owrecome o' some auld sang,
I never took tent, but an awsome chill on the heat o' my
    heart-strings fell,
    And I shook like a three days' bairn when she said,
        " He'll be, if there's naething gaes wrang."

V.

" If there's naething gaes wrang," quo' I tae mysel ten
    times in the coorse of the day,
    What nonsense is this I'm wastin' my heart tae cherish
        sae constant and keen ?
I'm certain that nocht can gae wrang wi' the lad, let him
    rove where he may,
    Aneth the blue dome o' the lift, in the howe o' the
        mountains sae green ;
But aft as I banished the gruesome thocht that follow'd
    the words like a shade,
    As aften the feelin' cam' till me unsocht, and wrocht
        on my mind like a spell,

Till substance could beir it na langer, and quatin' my
    darg at the spade,
And sayin', " I'm gaun tae meet Willie," I made for
    the road tae the hill.

VI.

A dour black clud owre the wedderglim darkent the lift
    and the glen,
  I kent it had shapit for something like this for nearly
    a fortnicht gane by,
But thocht it wad keepit a day or twa mair, else Willie
    wad need made a fen',
  Tae bide at the cottage contentit, and haud himsel'
    cosie and dry ;
For though it be nocht for a shepherd like me to be oot
    in the weet or the storm,
  Wi' never a bield frae the angry blash, but the bouk
    o' an auld grey cairn ;
Thae whitefaced toon's fowk gree far best wi' the air
    weel tempert and warm,
  And needs maun look after their tender hides like a
    shilpit lass or a bairn.

VII.

And weel did it heppen for me that day I carena'd for
    weather or win',
  For juist as I managed the Wingate brae-heid the
    black clud broke wi' a roar,
And a' doon Daur tae the Hass o' Benuff, wi' an unco-like
    deafenin' din ;

The claps o' the thunner seem'd chasin' ilk ither like
waves on a storm-lasht shore ;
And oot o' the mids' o' the collied lift richt doon on the
howe o' Petrail,
The reid jagg'd bolts o' the fireflaucht flichtert and
skirr'd alang,
And a lownness deeper than ocht but death had fa'n on
the mirksome dale,
Afore the big draps cam' tae the grun', and I thocht
on the something gaun wrang.

VIII.

" The Lord look efter my storm-sted lad, and haud him
a wee in Thy care ! "
My heart broke oot wi' the wilyart cry, as I saw, far
doon in the glen,
A something that lookt like the shape o' a man come
owre frae the dazzlet muir,
And crossin' Petrail at the Peden burnfit, come on
tae the hill at a sten' ;
I kent it was nane but the laddie I socht, in pairt by his
lassie-like gang,
As far frae the lamp o' the muirlan' herd as the mirk
is far frae the mune ;
And I thocht tae mysel', " Thank God for His care, he's
safe, and there's naething gane wrang,
And Jean'll be prood o' us baith this nicht, let oor
comin' be syne or sune."

IX.

But juist as the gled words loupt tae my lip a flash like
    a furnace gade by,
  And I trow'd that the lift wad be riven in bits by the
    horrible crack owreheid,
And the bolt o' the levin had whizzed sae close it left
    me birselt and dry,
  And the din o' the thunner had dung me sae I stood
    for the moment deid ;
And the first wild look I gat at the howm where Willie
    had ta'en tae the hill,
  The turf had been plewt wi' a fiery cou'ter deep as a
    drain in spring ;
And oot in the saft green hollow his corpse was streekit
    stiffly and still,
  And a' that was left o' my bonnie bairn was a blackent
    and gruesome thing.

X.

God o' the thunner! forgie me the aith that stertled the
    hills o' my hame,
  When I saw Thy creature, the pride o' my life, struck
    doon i' that fearsome day ;
I coo'r at the fit o' Thy gowden throne, and own wi' a
    heart o' shame,
  That my spirit gade up in a desperate word, mak's
    mortal rebellious tae say :
But Thou kens only—as ken Thou maun—that mair
    than my ain wild wae,

I thocht on the mither that sat by the ingle wi' heid
     boo't forrit tae hear
The fit that wad nevermair lichten her look as she heard
     it climbin' the brae,
  The voice that mair than a lover's vows had charms
     for her eager ear.

XI.

Thou kens, O Lord! what treasure was set on the young
     life nippet sae sune,
  Thou kens hoo bitter a weird Thy will has laid on us
     baith tae dree,
And Lord! Thou kens Thy servant's heart ne'er carps
     that Thy will be dune,
  Though the daein' o't whiles brings little but wae on
     mine as weel as on me:
And e'en as the knowledge o' a' that is can never be tint
     tae Thy sicht,
  And Thy strong richt airm that is swift tae strike is
     aften as swift tae save.
I bide in the faith that ae black blot 'll fade in the
     bleezin' licht
  That gies me a look o' my bonnie bairn on the tither
     side o' the grave.

XII.

I seldom can think on the wearifu' past—I maistly leeve
     in a dwawm;
  The ills o' the warl are little tae thole when the first
     sair bruilzie is bye,

And the terrible sicht, that day in the glen, has left me
    donart and calm,
  Sae calm that aften I ferlie sair gin the springs o' my
    passion be dry,
For even when Jeanie, my winsome wife, had follow'd
    her son to the grave,
  The never a tear-drap saftened my cheek, but aye like
    an auld auld sang
That weird ghaist murmur grew in my heart as dour as
    the sough o' the wave,
  And I ken that the best o' my life had en't when I
    grued at the "something wrang."

A SPRIG O' HEATHER.

I.

It cam' in the faulds o' a lovenote true—
    This sprig o' heather,
Straucht doon frae the mountains whaur it grew
    In the warm spring weather;
Fresh, wi' the fresh wild air o' the glens,
Dear, frae the dear young thing that kens
Hoo fain my wearifu' heart wad be
Tae bide wi' her ain on the muirland lea,
    Amang the heather.

II.

It brings me a glisk o' the hichts and howes
    Whaur grey mists gether,
Whaur blithe birds sing and the wee burn rows
    In the wilds o' heather;
The scent o' the sweet thing fills my min'
Like the croon o' an auld sang kent langsyne,
And my heart gangs back to the joyfu' days,
When its beat was licht as the breeze that strays
    Amang the heather.

III.

O bonniest gem o' the treeless wild !
    I carena whether,
As neither a flow'r nor a tree thou'rt styled,—
    Thou art dear as either :
And lang as the linty bigs her nest
In the bield o' thee on the mountain crest,
Sae lang will the muirlan' heart o' me
Hae a nameless joy it can only pree
    Amang the heather.

IV.

The lily sae mim or the blude-reid rose
    May charm anither,
But a Scotsman's heart in his bosom glows
    At the sicht o' heather ;
Whether it wave on the breezy hills,
And a' the air wi' its fragrance fills,
Or comes as a token that some sweet face
Is missin' his ain at the trystin' place
    Amang the heather.

V.

And oh, tae hae haud o' that face e'enoo !
    Row'd close thegither,
Where nocht but the sun e'er dichts the dew
    Frae the wavin' heather ;
Row'd close thegither aneth ae plaid
When lichts were gloamin' and winds were laid ;
And never a tongue but the bird's abune
Could speak o' the ferlies said or dune
    Amang the heather !

AUTUMN.

Lo ! the languid Summer lies
   Down upon her couch of pain,
And the look that's in her eyes
   Says she will not rouse again :
Tend her well, sweet love, for you
Will mourn her all the Winter through.

Was not this a wondrous web,
   Woof'd with happiness she wove,
Ere her power had reach'd the ebb,
   And her arm with Winter strove ?
But she claims the gift she gave
To fold around her in the grave.

We must yield, alas ! ye know,
   Ere the fields have lost their green,
I must with the Summer go
   Where the wave will roll between :
But, when birds again do sing,
I will come and crown the Spring.

UNFULFILLED RENOWN.

THE history of our island rings
    With praises of its great of old,
And slumbering loyalty upsprings
    Where'er their valiant deeds are told ;
With swelling heart and sparkling eye
We mouth the names that cannot die.

Their fight is fought, their victory won,
    Their meed is at the hands of fame ;
They win the wreath by what is done,
    And wear it, and no man can blame ;
Nor do we grudge the grateful praise
That wafts their name to later days.

But who shall say that on the roll
    Oblivion hides there was not one
As mighty ?—nay, a mightier soul,
    Than these dame Fortune smiled upon ?
A man whose single sword and shield
Had turned the chances of a field.

Who knew the weight and worth of will,
    And prized it as all leaders do ;

Nor lacked the aids of strength and skill
  To place him 'mong the favour'd few ;
But whose young fame and budding wreath
Were blasted in the frost of death.

While yet the horn was at the lip
  To sound his name through all the land,
One fatal moment wrought a slip,
  The horn fell from the faltering hand,
And the proud prelude's opening tone
Failed in an instant and was gone.

And in the flight of such a soul
  Our loss is greater than we know,
For victory's tide unchecked may roll,
  And mighty hearts still guide its flow ;
And so we hail their power with pride,
Unconscious that a greater died.

The bud that's nipt beneath the gale
  Might shape to show the fairer flower ;
But whoe'er thinks of buds that fail,
  When seated in the Summer bower,
Where those that braved the tempest stand,
And hallow all the fragrant land ?

So with the past ; great men enthrall
  The wondering gaze of after-time :
But seldom are the tears that fall
  For those who perished ere the prime.

We own their meed might not be less,
Yet yield a greater to success.

But in the world beyond the grave,
     Their guerdon will be rightly given ;
The unfought combats of the brave
     Shall work their recompense in heaven ;
And the nipt bud at last disclose
The beauties of the perfect rose.

TIRED.

COME to me, Sleep—for I am faint and worn;
  All night my brain hath divèd deep
For pearls of fancy to adorn
These waifs of song; until at morn,
Of all its eager impulse shorn,
  How willingly it comes to steep
  Its languor in the balm of sleep.

Come to me, Sleep—behold I cast away
  At last the book whose witching lore
Hath kept thee from thy rightful sway,
And made the night as rough as day
With toil; but thought no more will stay,
  Its wing that late could proudly soar,
  Droops, jaded with the strain it bore.

Come to me, Sleep—I have a traitor been,
  But now repentant crave thy kiss;
As lover woos who once has seen
His mistress wrongly slighted, lean
I now upon thy love serene,
  That sees through negligence like this,
  And yields at last its balmy bliss.

Come to me, Sleep—I yield thee up my soul,
    Do with it as thou wilt ; it seems
There are no arms like thine ; O fold
Them softly round my frame, and hold
My head upon thy bosom old ;
    For happiness my spirit deems
    Nowhere but in thy world of dreams.

O ! gentle Sleep, I feel thy kindly glow,
    I feel thy balmy presence near ;
Already faint the noises grow
That sound so fitfully below,
One after one the last lights go,
    And I who neither see nor hear
    Have comfort in another sphere.

A SONG OF PAIN.

Turn me aboot wi' my face to the wa',
    O mither, till I dee !
I canna look intae your een ava
    That wont to be dear tae me :
I want to be dune wi' the licht o' day
    And the weariesome fauchts o' life,
For little o' pleasure or promise hae they
    To the mither that ne'er was a wife.

Gie me a kiss or a heartenin' word,
    O mither, or I gang !
Ye mind hoo ye ca't me your winsome bird
    Lang syne when I kent nae wrang :
And never had I sic need o' your love
    In the far away time as noo :
I hae nane but yoursel' and the God above,
    Whase mercy I'm fley'd tae sue.

Comfort the bairn I'm leavin' ahin',
    O mither, when I'm gane !
The puir thing 'ill thole for his mither's sin
    As bitterly as his ain ;
And dinna be hard wi' his faither, min',
    Suld he come when I am awa',
But think on the joyfu' days lang syne,
    When he liket me best o' a' !

REAR OUR FLAG ON HIGH!

REAR our flag on high !
   That gift which Freedom gave,
'Twill stream above our victory,
   Or shroud us in the grave.
There's pride of heart and strength of arm
   Rank'd at the guns below,
And he that weens to work it harm
   Must be a dauntless foe.

Rear our flag on high !
   And when it flies unfurl'd,
Mark how it stands against the sky,
   And seems to dare the world !
The light winds proudly lift its folds
   And toss them far and free,
And forth the good ship fares, and holds
   Old England on her lee.

Pour your choicest wine,
   And pledge the vessel round,
And pray that she may plough the brine
   For years with timbers sound :

In peace or war, in shine or storm,
  Unconquered as of yore,
With England's banner standing firm
  Through all the tempest's roar.

Then, should Heav'n decree
  This flag of ours must fall,
In terror men may look to see
  The dismal end of all ;
And even in that hour 'twill seem,
  When sinks the vessel low,
To flutter on the 'whelming stream
  In triumph to the foe !

TINTOC-TAP.

AN OLD SAW, WITH A RUNNING COMMENTARY.

On Tintoc-tap there is a mist,
 (Gin ye misdoot me—gang and see ;)
And in the mist there is a kist,
 (A queer place for a kist tae be !)
And in the kist there is a caup,
 (As fine as e'er held barley-bree ;)
And in the caup there is a drap ;
 (A wee drap screigh, it seem'd tae me.)
Tak' up the caup and drink the drap,
 (If ye're a Scot, ye'll dae't wi' glee,)
And ye'll fa' doon on Tintoc-tap
 (Sic dule does every drunkard dree !)

EPISTLE TO NELLIE.

IN REPLY TO HERS IN THE *Friend* OF 18TH AUGUST.

THE English mail cam' in yestreen,
A welcome sicht for langin' een,
Wi' news o' mony a far-aff freen',
    Tae touch the hearts
That under weary exile grien
    In foreign parts.

I gat some paper wi't mysel',
Some business letters, sharp and fell ;
And ane that, by the very smell
    And grup thegither,
The toomest-heided loon could tell
    Was frae the heather.

Nane o' yer sma'lly, formal mites
A warldly chield in haste indites,
But siclike as a mither writes
    A son she loes—
Sax sheets, weel cross'd in black and white,
    And pang'd wi' news.

And though the sheets were lang and wide,
The cover yet had room tae hide
Ae scrap that gart me dance wi' pride,
   Richt fain, I tell ye—
A rhymin' note, fu' bravely tried,
   Frae ane ca'd Nellie.

She roos'd my hamely muirlan' skill
In stringin' blauds o' rhyme at will ;
But fear'd that lately I'd been ill,
   Or ceas'd tae min'
O' freens at hame, wha used tae fill
   My thochts langsyne.

"And wad I no," she'd kindly spier,
"For sake o' them wha loe'd tae hear,
Though far frae a' I reckon'd dear,
   And owre the main,
Juist kittle up my harp, and cheer
   Their hearts again ?"

I'm sure I needna blush tae tell
That I thocht meikle o' mysel'
When her sweet lines, sae frank and fell,
   I croon'd wi' care,
And heard her say she likit well
   My rhymin' ware.

And, by my word, I'll dae my best
Tae grant the lass her sma' request ;

I'll court the muse, and never rest
    Till she be kin',
And screed me aff some fancy, drest
    In language fine.

Meantime, dear Nellie, never fear
That ocht I ever see or hear
Can quench the deathless love, I bear
    For Scotia's shore,
Or for the freen's sae leal an' dear
    In days o' yore.

I've seen Niagara's waters dashing
In headlong fury—roaring—splashing,
And Montmorency's torrent crashing
    Its rocks below,
While high in heaven the spray was flashing,
    A burnished bow.

But though the sichts and soun's be grand
That greet me in this noble land,
I'd niffer a' for that lane strand
    Attour the sea ;
Oh, airt me hame tae auld Scotland,
    Ye powers that be !

And when I sing, as I hae said,
Thinkna the scene will e'er be laid
Save in the kintra o' the plaid
    And bonnet blue,
Whaur man is bauld, and wife and maid
    Are leal and true.

A GUST ON THE LAKE.

YESTERDAY I lay at rest
In the heather upon the mountain's breast
And watch'd the little lake below
Unmov'd by tidal ebb or flow ;
Mirror'd in which high Heaven was seen
With all its flecks and bars between—
A beauteous sight ; a sight to give
Delight as long as one might live,
For years of toil will not efface
    The memory of that winsome scene ;
The stillness of the lonely place,
    The perfect peace, the calm serene.

Suddenly out of the mountain gorge
A wandering wind its way did urge :
It came from white clouds far away ;
It was only a gust—and it did not stay,
But it smote the face of the little lake,
And the beauteous mirror shiver'd and brake.
It was only a gust—and it soon pass'd on,
But the glamour that fill'd the glen had gone ;
And long did I linger on the hill
    And watch, with desire that was almost pain,
Ere the troubled heart of the lake was still,
    And peace return'd to her home again.

A storm surged up in my mind to-day
An angry storm—but it did not stay,
A slanderous whisper had swept the glen,
And stirr'd the blood of the mountain men ;
And mine too rose,—but I went apart
And commun'd in solitude with my heart ;
And I said " O heart ! wilt never learn
The lessons that face thee at every turn ?
Hast thou forgotten the little lake
    That slumber'd so sweetly yesterday,
And yet how swiftly the storm did take
    Its fairy beauty and peace away ?

" The storms and eddies that vex the world
Will keep thee ever in torture whirl'd
If like the little mountain lake,
The impress of each wind thou dost take.
But the mind of a man should meet the storm,
Nor take from the blustering tempest harm ;
Glassy and calm its face should show
No matter how fiercely the whirlwinds blow ;
And only resemble the lake in this :—
    That in all seasons it lowly lies,
At peace with itself and all that is,
    Reflecting the calm of its natal skies."

Miscellaneous Sonnets.

POESIE.

WHENCE comes the charm that broods along thy shore,
   O sunny land of song ?   What potent thrall,
   Reckless of ocean's rise, or flow, or fall,
Holds us about thy marge for evermore ?
Here, where the long wave breaks in measured time,
   And fills our being with its rhythmic moan,
   From far inland the glories of thy zone
Burst on our view, and beckon us to climb.
Shades of the mighty dead ! whose snowy towers
   Stud the deep gorges and the wooded braes,
Is there no nook for cots so small as ours ?
   No tree whereof we yet might gather bays ?
But to be with thee, and to hear the wave
Roll music round the land, is all we crave.

LOVE.

WHERE is the height at which the poet's soul
  Will cease to soar ? beneath the boundless sky,
  By sea or shore peaks do not point so high
But it may scale ; or by the frigid roll
Of Greenland's waters, or the desert lone
  Of utmost Ind ; in calm, or cloud, or storm,
  Earth opens to its " sesame " kind and warm
The hidden beauties of its every zone.
Then with a limitless survey like this
  Tell me, my heart ! what magic doth thee thrall
  That thou canst find a comfort more than all
Earth's wonders yield in one slight maiden's kiss ?
O reckless heart ! dost think thou findest there
The charm that keepeth these forever fair ?

FAME.

In the cool watches of the silent night
　　My soul was wafted to the land of dreams
And moved in ecstacy of calm delight
　　Along the margin of its silver streams.
With raptured eye it saw the bright array
　　Of goodly gifts for mortals held in store,
　　And, faint with passion, hunger'd more and more
To win some token of its favoured stay.
"Choose what thou wilt," a passing voice did call;
　　At once my spirit made a snatch at Fame,
But with the bauble in its grasp did fall,
　　Nor ever after could its ground reclaim.
Alas! that wish of mine should yearn to clasp
A gawd that brings such troubles to the grasp.

APRIL.

THERE'S not a month in all the rolling year
  So true to life as April ; sun and shower
  Change rule so quickly that the trembling flower
Begins to smile before it sheds the tear.
In me as well some darker hours of fear
  Mix with the lightsome joy that fills the day,
But less and less these cloudy thoughts appear,
  Sweet winds of hope do waft them all away ;
Already in my soul the breath that brings
  The bud and blossom has been gently blown ;
  And at its touch awaken'd thought has grown
Beyond the limit of these sluggish springs :
So blow, sweet wind ! and clear the sky above
And all my soul will blossom o'er with love.

BANISHED.

As some lone dweller in a distant land
  Chooseth to linger by the restless sea,
  And counts the leagues of shifting waves that be
Between him and his home, while fancy's wand
Brings for one moment to his gloating view
  The happy times that he can know no more,
Then blinds him, weeping—till each scene he knew
  Fades on his eye along the dismal shore,—
So I, forever banished from thy presence, feel
  A momentary gladness in the thought
  That eyes so bright as thine at one time brought
Heaven down to me, and glow'd to list my weal.
Alas! for broader than the exile's sea
'S the gulf now stretched between those eyes and me.

HEROISM.

Not only in the time and garb of war
   The hero breathes ; not only now and then
   We catch bright glimpses of this man of men,
The labour of whose hands is nois'd afar ;
But even now, in these degenerate days,
   As noble hearts do beat as those that bore
   The invader backward in the days of yore,
And earn'd the guerdon of a deathless praise.
Wherever human hearts do war with wrong,
   Or maiden virtue shuns the fowler's guile,
Where honest hands to humble toil belong,
   Or wealth assists the trodden poor to smile—
There throbs a soul which wins the highest claim
To ring—remembered—in the song of Fame !

DISCONTENT.

THERE'S not a bliss in all the joys we clip
　　Can match the charm of those in whose rich glow
　　We clothe the future—joys we never know,
Yet long so much to finger that we slip
Substantial pleasures lying round our feet,
　　For these same glimpses, beckoning far away,
Which, when we chase, as speedily retreat:
　　No charm we hold can bid their brightness stay.
We reach the spot where all was deemed so fair.
　　From yon far mountain where we made our moan,
　　But ah! the gleam that lit the land is gone,
And the lone moorland stretches waste and bare:
　　While onward still, amid the gathering gloom,
　　Flits the weird glow that wiles us to the tomb!

SINGING.

To-DAY I heard a singer in the crowd
  Discourse sweet melody, and could not choose
  But stand and listen ; for that she did use
The gift she bore by Nature's hand endowed
So sweetly, and her notes both low and loud
  Thrill'd with such passion that I could not pass,
But paused, half conscious that my heart avowed
  A sudden yearning for the comely lass :
And in that thrill of sympathy I knew
  That here was one whose maiden soul was flung
  In all its richness thro' the lay she sung,
And here, if still on earth, one heart was true ;
And mine had been apart from such so long
It bless'd the wanderer for her welcome song !

ROMANCE.

O THAT some touch of elfin power might glance
   Along the strings of this my lowly lyre!
   That more than mortal ardour might inspire
This song of mine to thee, far-famed Romance!
Lone land, upon whose tracts no sun doth beam
   That heats our nether globe, though faint and far
   The mellowed lustre of one drowsy star
Yet haunts thy limit with its hallowing gleam—
(The star of song).   Against thy faery shore
   Its rays are rolled, as the long tide is rolled
Against the unconscious beach for evermore;
   While we—rapt watchers—through the gloom behold
Thy wondrous heights, and long therein to soar,
   And scatter broadcast all the gems they hold.

REALITY.

STAR-STRUCK, and throbbing with such thoughts as these
   I turned me towards the town ; for all night long
   With poet frenzy I had timed my song
To the deep swinging of the listless seas.
And O, my God ! what creatures found I there
   To listen lore like this ; in vice grown bold
   And misery mad, their haggard features told
Their higher need. My dream dissolved in air,
And in its stead this thought engrossed my mind—
   That if the poet's mission be to bring
Earth nearer Heaven, a way more sure and kind
   Than prating starry nonsense is to fling
One ray of light upon the wretched, blind,
   Seared souls that thread the dark streets grovelling.

LOVE-WEARY.

WHAT shall I do (love being dead) to bring
  Back to my heart the rapture and the joy,
  The glorious fancies of the dreaming boy
That made my early life eternal spring?
Red lips, soft eyes, the spell of woven arms—
  All these have failed, embraces are grown cold.
  Eyes thrill me not as they were wont of old,
Nor at the red lips' touch my bosom warms.
I am love-weary; come, O radiant Spring,
  And in the lonely places wake delight,
For I at large would fain be wandering
  With thy glad presence evermore in sight;
Thence might I turn upon the world to prove
Thy touch doth make a substitute for love.

SPRING.

Who has not felt thy witching presence, Spring?
   Upon the mountain top and in the glen
   Thy rapid coming is foretold to men
In diverse ways : the wandering breezes fling
Gladness around us in our outs and ins :
   Aloft, the opening sky is deeply blue,
   And the bright orb of morning glistening through
Smiles on the fearless songster that begins
To hail thy reign : the earth, no longer coy,
   Arrays herself as might a beauteous bride,
While smiles and songs of mirth reveal the joy
   And fulness of her wondrous mother-pride.
O happy man unto whose heart these bring
The dewy freshness of thy spirit, Spring !

G I F T S .

IF I unto my kindred dust should go,
  With but one gift of fortune, and that gift
  Of my own choosing, do ye think I'd lift
A longing eye on wealth, or worldly show,
Or beauty, or the higher meeds of fame ?
  No ! one by one I'd set these gifts aside
  As scarce worth having, and with poet-pride
I'd wreathe this chaplet round my deathless name :
One little song—one little rapturous lay,
  Simple, perhaps, and sad, but true to all
The best in Nature, of which men would say,
  " Here truly is a charm whose linkèd thrall
We may not break—it breathes the heart's pure play,
  And till this ends it cannot pass away."

PLEDGED.

FRIENDS, I have sworn a vow. The terrible bond
　That Jephtha, flush'd with vict'ry, register'd
　Was not one whit more certain to be heard
And sealed in heaven, than this one now beyond
My revocation ; and although to his,
　In point of magnitude or pain to keep,
　Mine be as streamlet to the boundless deep,
Yet, calmly pondered, it amounts to this—
That in the judgment of Almighty God
　And interest of my particular soul,
　This bond requires fulfilment just as whole
And faithful as that found : therefore beware
　Lest ye should swerve me from the narrow road,
And mar a heavenly covenant unaware.

NATURE.

THE sweetest intercourse of kindred souls
   Is not all sweet: harsh words will intervene
   To mar their joy, as o'er the blue serene
Italian heaven a black cloud often rolls,
Flinging long glooms on earth; so all that springs
   'Tween man and man at best is incomplete;—
   Bitters flow close upon his choicest sweet,
And love, like riches, is not void of wings.
But with the constancy that doth belong
   To every motion of the moon-drawn sea
   My heart is led in willing thrall of thee—
Spirit of Nature, whose sole voice is song!
In whose pure love nor hitch nor flaw doth bide,
But rolls for ever an unbroken tide.

L'ENVOI.

DEAR Jack, the posie is made up I pull'd—
  The wild hill blossoms wrought in wilder rhyme;
  Is there aught in it has the scent of thyme
And freshness of the moors? or has my spirit, school'd
In deadening cities, lost the power to throw
  Their natural charms around the scenes we love?
Mayhap it has; yet would I have thee know,
  Nature was still my theme; the gentle dove
Mourns not her absent mate with moan more sad
  Than I, pent in the smoke these cheery days
  At losing her; and O if any lays
Of mine do breathe her music, I am glad!
And in contentment leave them at thy feet,
Knowing thy heart will own that music sweet.

JAMES MORGAN.

(Inscribed, with affectionate regards, to James Morgan, Jr.)

WEEP not for him, thy dear one gone to rest ;
  Weep not for him,—he hath no need of tears :
  But if the dismal future's emptier years
Appal thee, then relieve thy laden breast
For sole self-comfort ; they that mourn are blest.
  Little *he* recks of all thy anxious fear ;
  He hath obey'd the edict of the spheres,
And lacks not pity, ev'n Love's tenderest.

This was no sapling, broken of the storm
  An hour before its time ; nay, but a goodly tree,
That in the light uprear'd its noble form,
  And to the winds spread out its branches free ;
And full of years, to mother earth has come
  Ripe, as a sheaf of wheat at harvest home !

THE LAST ENEMY.

How will he take me,—this dread foe,—and when?
   Will he assail me in the noonday light,
   Bearing down on me in embattl'd might,
And sweep me from the ways and gaze of men?
Or in the solitude of some deep glen
   Will he, when I am far from human sight,
   Creeping upon me like a thief at night,
Stab in the dark and drag me to his den?
What matters it? I neither know nor care.
   Come he like Judas with his false embrace,
Or seeking to o'erwhelm me with his air :
   Indifferent alike to time and place
His dart I'll welcome with my bosom bare,
   And fearless, yield me ; smiling in his face.

REST.

COMING—he knows not whence, and going soon—
 He knows not where ; uncertain of his years ;
 Certain of nought, alas ! save toil and tears—
Tears in the night and weary toil at noon—
What profiteth a man Life's doubtful boon ?
 What recompense is there for all his fears ?
 His slavish terror of the despot spheres ?
And all his thousand woes beneath the moon ?
There is but one : only the great sweet Rest
 To which he hasteth ; sweet it needs must be
 When fretted with the life-long bondage, he,
Like a tired infant on its mother's breast
Shuts weary eyes, and from life's fading strand
Follows his fathers to the silent land.

I WOO'D MY LOVE.

I woo'd my love in the merry spring time,
   And O ! sae cheery sang the laverock frae the sky ;
Wi' the world fair before me and my spirit in its prime,
   Never laverock held a heicher head than I.

I won my love in the lang simmer day,
   And O ! sae sweetly sang the lintie on the lea,
An' my heart—as blithe's the lintie's—had but little
      thocht o' wae—
   Heaven seemed tae ope its gowden gates to me.

I lost my love in the dowie back-en',
   And O ! sae sadly sang the mavis on the hill :
Hoo I warslet through the autumn by mysel' I hardly
      ken,
   Never herriet mavis dreept sae lane and chill.

I mourn my love a' the hale winter through,
   And O ! sae lanely sings the snawbird in the snaw ;
But the bird will whistle bonnie when the simmer sky
      is blue,
   And my weary heart maun break, or hear it a' !

WINTER.

I CANNA thole the breeze that springs
   Ayont the wastlin' sea,
Its lown saft music only flings
   A dowie dwawm on me ;
Far liefer wad I hear the blast
   Roar owre the norlan' main,
For Winter's fury smoors the past,
   And lea's me man again.

In pleasure's lap I lay and slum'd
   The leelang simmer through,
Where nocht but weeds o' idless blum'd,
   And the whimprin' wast win' blew.
But like some moth, attour the slugh
   I lap at Winter's ca',
And leuch tae hear his lanesome sugh
   Come thro' the driftin' snaw.

Then blaw thou blast, baith lood and snell,
   Thy breath but wauks my glee ;
The reid blude risin' frank and fell,
   Comes dinlin' tae my bree.
And on the stey storm-blaudit hill
   Defying nicht and thee,
I gether mair o' wit and will
   Than simmer e'er could gie.

IN LOVE.

I THINK of thee, when morn bestows
Her kiss upon the waking rose ;
When song-birds carol, clear and loud,
High up beside the sunny cloud :
And sure those sights and sounds so rare,
The very freshness in the air,
Give new delight and joy to me,
Born of the touch they take from thee.

I live for thee, when man with man
Is working out the fated plan ;
When fears and hopes, and woes and joys
Distract the sense with jarring noise ;
And in the melee, ringed with foes,
More fiercely fall my eager blows,
Because that in the end I see
Their weight will hew my way to thee.

I dream of thee—when night hath hung
Her chain upon the gladsome tongue
That cheer'd us in the rosy dawn,
When light was clear on lake and lawn :
And though the dreams that come be sweet
As ever fell at mortal's feet,
I fling them from me, glad and free,
And wake again to life and thee.

FAREWEEL.

I.

I'M leavin' thy gray glens, Wanlock,
　Wi' a heavy heart and sair ;
I'm sayin' Fareweel to the dear auld hills
　I'll aiblins see nae mair :
The bee may come back to the heather blumes,
　And the crake to the clover lea ;
But the hinny and perfume a' are gane
　That hae drawn me aft to thee !

II.

I've been to the green braes, Wanlock,
　That rang wi' oor youthfu' glee ;
I've keekit ance mair at the slee wee neuk
　Where my first luve trystit me :
I've boo't my heid on the cauld heid-stane
　Where the kindly auld folks lie ;
And I've grutten sair at the herriet nest
　That was hingin' empty by.

III.

It's waesome wark this, Wanlock,
  Takin' leave o' the things we lo'e;
It's this that whitens the haffet locks,
  And runkles the brentest broo;
And it's seldom we meet in oor later years,
  'Mang their pleisures and their pain,
The freenships rare, and the leal true luves
  We kent i' the days bygane.

IV.

The whaup i' thy mirk lift, Wanlock,
  Has skirl'd me a wild Fareweel;
The bonnie wee lintie sabbit sair
  As she cour't in her heathery biel':
And ilka bit floo'r on the lanesume heichts
  Had a blab o' weet in its e'e,
As tho' it bude greet at the cruel fate
  That was pairtin' it and me.

V.

I've spiel'd thy stey heichts, Wanlock,
  For the hinmaist time I troo;
I'll dauner nae mair by the wimplin' burn,
  Nor rest on the mountain's broo;
For I'm aff and awa to the wastlin' warl'
  Where my wife and bairnies bide;
And I'll never set fit i' thy boun's again,
  At dawin' or gloamin'-tide!

VI.

But in that far hame, Wanlock,
   I'll aften sit at e'en,
And muse on the joys I've tasted here
   Wi' monie a trusty freen ;
And I'll bless ilk honest heart that bides
   I' thy cots sae bien and sma' ;
And the auld kirkyaird i' the howe, that hides
   The dearest hearts o' a' !

Appendix.

TO ROB WANLOCK.

(Author of " Moorland Rhymes," now in Canada.)

BY ALEXANDER G. MURDOCH.

BRIGHT Wanlock ! master of the moorland harp,
　Whose clear and fine-toned melody recalls
　The open moors, with woods and waterfalls,
And breezy uplands—outlined, clear, and sharp ;
　Thou worthiest of our living Doric bards.
I bring the tribute of my muse to thee,
　My swimming eyes in fancy turn'd towards
Thy new-found home across the wave-strown sea !
　Canadian Scots, who love the muse's swell,
　　Wreathe ye a chaplet for his poet brow,
　That he, once more song-taken, wild and well,
　　May thus redeem his early honour'd vow,
And win a guerdon nobler than a crown—
The heritage of a fulfill'd renown.

TO ROB WANLOCK.

(Found among the papers of the late Lord Macaulay, and supposed to be first draft of " The Battle of Lake Regillus.")

BY ALEXANDER ANDERSON ("SURFACEMAN.")

THE rough Lars Andersonius,
　By the nine gods he swore,
That he would go to Glasgow
　And see his friends once more.
He swore by pick and shovel,
　He swore by ink and quill,
He swore by the nine Muses
　On the Parnassian Hill ,
He swore by all the goodly tomes
　That he would yet indite,
That he would see Murdochius,
Stewardus and Wanlochius,
　And grasp their hands full tight.

So he sent letters east and west,
　He sent them far away,
He sent one to Stewardus.
　Where rolls the lordly Tay ;

He sent one to Wanlochius,
 Bleak Wanlock's boast and pride,
He sent one to Murdochius,
 The bard by Clutha's side.
And each and all he bound them,
 And how could they refuse?
To meet him at Dunlop Street,
 And battle for the Muse.

The rough Lars Andersonius,
 When he had sworn this vow,
He girded on his armour,
 And helmed his massive brow.
He called for pick and shovel,
 To serve as sword and shield,
He called for his war-chariot,
 And proudly took the field.

Hurrah for the bright shovel
 In a strong navvy's hand,
Hurrah for the wide whirling pick
 That heads the rugged band;
Hurrah for the war-chariot,
 That hath a heart of flame,
And clanks along on iron feet,
 On pathways of the same.

By many a tower and hamlet
 Snorted his mighty steed,
He sprang from echoing hill to hill,
 Nor halted in his speed;

Men sprang from his dread pathway,
And maidens ran away,
While in their fear they questioned
" Who rides so fast to-day ? "
But on went Andersonius,
Nor looked he back on home,
But cried, " He cannot ride too fast
Who rides to FRIENDS and ROME."

MY DEAR WANLOCK,—Will leave here on Friday night, and
reach Dunlop St. somewhere about 8.20. Can you be on the
platform ? I expect Murdoch there.

A. ANDERSON ("Surfaceman").

P.S.—This in great haste.

TO ROB WANLOCK.

BY NISBET NOBLE.

BOLD singer, 'neath thy ringing tones our being all is
    stirred ;
We feel thy soul in every thought, thy heart in every
    word ;
Be it of moorland loves thy song, or rising bold and
    grand,
It sweeps away on eagle's wings across our mountain
    land ;
Our hearts grow grit, our pulses beat, fierce as becomes
    the free ;
And bounding to our throbbing feet we greet thee o'er
    the sea ;
Here 'mid the hills we chant thy lays, and crags and
    cliffs give voice ;
We croon them on the heathery braes, and woods and
    winds rejoice ;
The moorland tarn, the mountain burn, the stirring
    strains have known ;
The echoes, warring clouds, return with voices of their
    own.

Sing on, sing on, for all the land from rugged shore to
    shore
Is thrilling with the notes that come three thousand
    miles or more ;
The spirits of the past are up, their viewless forms speed
    by,
And pour from Freedom's flowing cup its nectar from on
    high.
The grey old cairns seem to move their blood-cemented
    stones ;
Dead heroes stir—we think we hear the rattling of their
    bones ;
Such magic words it was that made them bear the trench-
    ant brand
In those far days when death and dool swept o'er our
    stricken land.

Canadian soil may claim thy form, but still thy heart we
    know
Is where the Highland heather blooms, and Scottish
    thistles grow ;
Each line of our historic page is open to thine eye ;
Thou mark'st the Northmen's ravens rage, the Roman
    eagles fly ;
And England's men-at-arms sweep on before thy eager
    ken,
And Bruce and Wallace rise from sleep, and tread the
    hills again.

And lo! around thee where thou art the hillsmen's spirits
    rise ;
The bloody heights of Abraham mayhap have met thine
    eyes ;
Canada's silent solitudes have heard the bagpipes' wail ;
And through her trackless woods hath rung the slogan
    of the Gael.
We know thou hear'st the ringing tones of merry
    mountain maids ;
And feel thy leal Scotch heart grow grit at sight of tartan
    plaids ;
Track after track of hill and glen now greets our sad
    eyes here ;
Swept of their warlike warrior men to feed the sheep
    and deer.
The bones and sinews of our hills are thrust across the
    brine ;
Their horny hands and iron wills, Canada, now are thine ;
The big, broad breast that gave them room, that room
    shall ne'er regret ;
The wilds and wilderness shall bloom beneath their
    footprints yet.

Hail to thee, brother bard ! To thee and such as thee
    belong,
O'er those far miles of pathless sea, a bright new realm
    of song :
Strong arms are there and earnest hearts, that fear nor
    force nor foes,
See how the forest giants reel beneath their sturdy blows;

17

And cities rise where erst the feet of the lone Indian
  trod,
And his fierce Manatow hath fled before the Christian's
  God.
The ploughman's whistle charms the ear where war-
  whoops shocked the skies,
And o'er the buried tomahawk the harvest riches rise :
And there, where swept the light canoe, the mighty
  steamship rides,
The churning waters deep and blue foam fierce around
  its sides ;
The solitary savage stands, with awed and wondering
  glance,
As civilization's teeming bands resistlessly advance ;
And, plunging in his woods again, he tells the wondrous
  tale
Beside the camp fire's lurid glare, and dusky cheeks
  grow pale.

And ere the tale is done they hear the clearing axe's
  sound—
The voices of the pioneers fill all the wilds around.
Where can he fly to shun their gaze ? when will their
  march be done ?
Ne'er till adown far distant days the whole fair land is
  won.
What though he chafe and rise in wrath, and rush in
  reckless ire
Along war's ruthless, blood-red path, and light the land
  with fire ;

The grim-browed borderer replies with deadly rifle
sound,
And soon his tented village lies all trampled on the
ground.
Away, away, far inland yet, their homeless way they
wage,
And mourn the fatal day they met, and woke the white
man's rage.

O ! civilization, many a crime thy name hath fathered,
lust
And rapine load the tides of Time o'er thy down-trodden
dust ;
The message of the Prince of Peace the heathen laugh
to scorn ;
We bore the Bible o'er the seas, then blared the bugle
horn,
And all the dogs of war let loose, untutored hearts to
move,
With sword and brand to understand the mysteries of
Love.

From here to yon Canadian strand, up, singers, all arise,
See Wanlock, thy adopted land, uplifts her pleading
eyes,
And bids thee tune thy voice to song, until the ringing
chords
Of earth's great heart swell out in wrath at thy indignant
words.

A grander theme has never yet awoke the poet's strain,
Though avarice may frown or fret, let Truth and Justice
    reign.

All hail! again, far distant bard, to grasp thy hand in
    mine
I'd gladly leave our storied land, and hie me o'er the
    brine ;
But I am powerless all, yet still, in spirit I can take
A friendly clasp, and every hill will keep thy name
    awake ;
And I can hear thy voice within the *Friend's* clear pages
    sound,
There, though thy manly face be hid—we meet on com-
    mon ground.

EPISTLE TO ROB WANLOCK (REID).

(Author of "Moorland Rhymes.")

BY JOHN ARBORY.

Hail ! brither bard attour the sea !
A hamely auld Scots sang frae thee,
Blythe wi' thy ain wee lintie's glee,
     I'd suner hae
Than hauf the rhymin' ware ye see
     In prent this day.

Aft hae I croon'd that winsome lay—
The lichtsome bird, the benty brae,
The gowd-broom touch'd and ting'd wi' blae,
     Abune—the lift
Cauld wi' the licht o' closing day,
     O' sun bereft.

And yon weird blink o' sang divine,
The weary dree o' " Auld Langsyne,"
Soughs owre the waefu' wanderer's min',
     Boo'd doon wi' cares—
I ferly gin sic fate be thine,
     Bard o' the muirs.

When eerie whaups, adoon the win',
Their lanely cry sen' driftin' in,
Frae moss an' fell—owre hag an' linn,
   I think o' thee,
Ne'er sichtin' hill or barren whin
    On muirlan' lea.

And e'en when heather blumes are young,
I miss the music o' thy tongue ;
Sae sweetly aye thy lyre was strung,
   Sae pawky—slee,
The hamert heart was douner't dung,
    An' dim't the e'e.

But, aiblins yet, for wha can tell ?
When simmer blauds the burstin' bell,
We'll welcome back thy singin' sel'
   To Wanlock gray,
And sweetest flowers suld deck the dell
    That bonny day.

Scotland, Aug., 1879.

TO ROB WANLOCK.

BY WALTER CHISHOLM.

SWEET singer o' the breezy hills
  Where grows the purple heather,
Where wimplin' rowe the muirlan' rills,
  And grey mists aften gether;
A verse or twa to let ye ken
  Hoo weel your ditties please me,
I here indite wi' rhymin' pen,
  An' trust ye will excuise me.

Whene'er your heather sprigs ye twine
  In fresh poetic posies,
I hum as lang frae line to line
  As bees 'mang bloomin' roses.
Altho' your face I ne'er hae seen
  I aiblins yet may see it,
Weel wad I like to ca' ye freen
  If fate wad sae decree it.

I am a heather bird mysel',
  And weel I loe the mountains,
The yellow furze that decks the fells,
  The moss that cleeds the fountains;

An' tho' the noo I've bad adieu
  To ilka charm o' Nature,
Wi' memory's e'e I still can view
  Their ilka form an' feature.

Adieu ! an' may your sweet-voiced muse
  Ne'er jilt ye nor forsake ye,
May still her freaks your fancy roose,
  An' up Parnassus take ye ;
An' while ye lilt o' plaidies grey,
  An' lovers happ'd thegither,
Let critics say whate'er they may—
  Ne'er slicht the hills o' heather !

TO ROB WANLOCK, MONTREAL.

BY NELLIE.

A HAMELY lilt, in hamely rhyme,
    I pen wi' heartsome glee,
To thee, sweet bard of Wanlock Glen,
    Across the Atlantic Sea.

It comes frae ane wha canna boast
    O' classical book lore,
But frae a heart that lo'es thy lilts,
    And cons them o'er an' o'er.

On freen's in bonnie Scotland
    You've surely ceased to min',
Wha lo'ed your moorland rhymes sae weel
    In days o' auld langsyne.

Oh! Wanlock's Muse, I pray you come,
    Roun' him a halo fling,
That he may joyously burst forth
    An' sweetly, gladly sing.

18

Dear Wanlock, in your far off hame,
 Hear my request sae sma'.
An' write some verses for the *Friend*,
 Altho' you're far awa'.

www.ingramcontent.com/pod-product-compliance
Lightning Source LLC
Chambersburg PA
CBHW030338270326
41926CB00009B/884